Assessment of Sexual Function: A Guide to Interviewing

Assessment of Sexual Function: A Guide to Interviewing

Formulated by the
Committee on Medical Education

Group for the Advancement of Psychiatry

Jason Aronson, New York

LIBRARY OF CONGRESS CATALOGING IN PUBLICATION DATA

Group for the Advancement of Psychiatry. Committee
on Medical Education.
Assessment of sexual function.

Bibliography: p.
1. Sex (Psychology). 2. Interviewing in psychiatry.
I. Title. [DNLM: 1. Interview, Psychological.
2. Sex behavior. HQ21 G88a 1974]
BF692.G75 1974 616.6   73-17781
ISBN 0-87668-128-3

Manufactured in the United States of America

TABLE OF CONTENTS

Table of Contents

Assessment of Sexual Function: A Guide to Interviewing

STATEMENT OF PURPOSE

THE GROUP FOR THE ADVANCEMENT OF PSYCHIATRY has a membership of approximately 300 psychiatrists, most of whom are organized in the form of a number of working committees. These committees direct their efforts toward the study of various aspects of psychiatry and the application of this knowledge to the fields of mental health and human relations.

Collaboration with specialists in other disciplines has been and is one of GAP's working principles. Since the formation of GAP in 1946 its members have worked closely with such other specialists as anthropologists, biologists, economists, statisticians, educators, lawyers, nurses, psychologists, sociologists, social workers, and experts in mass communication, philosophy, and semantics. GAP envisages a continuing program of work according to the following aims:

1. To collect and appraise significant data in the field of psychiatry, mental health, and human relations;
2. To reevaluate old concepts and to develop and test new ones;
3. To apply the knowledge thus obtained for the promotion of mental health and good human relations.

GAP is an independent group, and its reports represent the composite findings and opinions of its members only, guided by its many consultants.

ASSESSMENT OF SEXUAL FUNCTION: A GUIDE TO INTERVIEWING was formulated by the Committee on Medical Education, which acknowledges on page 763 the participation of various GAP members and Fellows, of consultants and others in the preparation of this report. The current members of this committee as well as all other committees and the officers of GAP are listed below.

COMMITTEE ON MEDICAL EDUCATION
Saul I. Harrison, Ann Arbor, Chr.
Raymond Feldman, Boulder, Colo.
David R. Hawkins, Charlottesville
Harold I. Lief, Philadelphia

John E. Mack, Chestnut Hill, Mass.
David S. Sanders, Los Angeles
Robert Alan Senescu, Albuquerque, N.M.
Bryce Templeton, Philadelphia
Paul Tyler Wilson, Bethesda, Md.

1

COMMITTEE ACKNOWLEDGMENTS

The Committee on Medical Education formulated this report under the chairmanship of David R. Hawkins, currently a member of the Committee. At that time three other members of GAP were also members of the Committee: Robert S. Daniels; William L. Peltz, currently a member of the Committee on Therapy; and Roy M. Whitman, currently a member of the Committee on International Relations.

Having decided to work toward a contribution to improve sexual education in medical schools, the Committee first undertook self-education of its members in order to assess the demands, attitudes and problems surrounding sexual matters which the physician is likely to encounter in this time of social change. In this learning phase many individuals from a number of institutions gave substantial and greatly appreciated help.

William Masters and Virginia Johnson consulted with the Committee and then invited its members to spend a day at the Reproductive Biology Research Foundation. Through their kindness our committee members became acquainted with their basic research as well as the techniques they employ in interviewing and treating marital units disturbed by sexual dysfunction.

At the same time, the preeminent position of *Playboy Magazine* as a purveyor of information about sexual matters to the general public led us to consultation with its publisher, Hugh Hefner, who graciously hosted one of the Committee's conferences in the Playboy headquarters. In addition, Nat Lehrman, senior editor, and others from *Playboy Magazine* furnished considerable helpful insight.

Paul Gebhard and other members of the Institute for Sex Research, Inc., at the University of Indiana hosted the Committee for a most instructive visit to the research center founded by the late Alfred C. Kinsey. On a number of occasions the Division of Family Study of the University of Pennsylvania Department of Psychiatry made available its facilities and staff, with great benefit to the Committee.

Among those who served as consultants are Mary Ann Bartusis, John Gagnon, John Mudd, Carol Nadelson, Barney V. Pisha, Wardell Pomeroy, David Reed, Sharon Satterfield, and Walter Shervington. Mary Calderone and Clark Vincent were among those who graciously read our penultimate draft and made useful criticisms. Members of the AMA Committee on Human Sexuality kept us up to date on the progress of that Committee's book, HUMAN SEXUALITY, and gave us the advantage of reading it in draft form.

The two Ginsburg Fellows, Stephen Ettenson and William R. Nadel, assigned the Committee on Medical Education, contributed most helpfully in the formulation of the report, and at the eleventh hour Warren J. Gadpaille, a member of GAP's Committee on Adolescence, amplified in an interesting and useful way the material on adolescence.

Finally, it would have been impossible to have pulled all this material together without the invaluable editorial assistance of Virginia Kennan.

To these and others who helped in so many ways we are grateful.

INTRODUCTION

This report by the Committee on Medical Education of the Group for the Advancement of Psychiatry is designed as a manual for the practicing physician, the medical student, and others in the health field. We have attempted a comprehensive discussion of interviewing as a means of evaluating the patient's sexual function and attitudes. In doing so, we cite selected clinical situations illustrative of instances in which the patient's sexual history is relevant to his condition.

It was apparent that in any succinct review of this diversified and complex field some readers would note deficiencies, but it is our hope that this book will provide a useful framework to be filled in from the reader's own knowledge and experience, which constitute a necessary background for its successful use as a guide.

Sometimes sexual problems mask underlying psychological conflicts. It is important to detect and to understand these conflicts before focusing primarily on the sexual problem itself. This book was formulated with the purpose of facilitating the task of the professional in identifying these conflicts.

1

SOME DOs AND DON'Ts FOR THE INTERVIEWER

Encouraged by the growing willingness of our society to examine and discuss openly the personal aspects of living, the medical profession has at last begun seriously to consider its responsibility for dealing with sexual behavior and sexual problems. A sober self-scrutiny within the medical community has revealed that the average physician, commonly believed to be an authority on human sexuality—and certainly the person most frequently consulted about sexual problems—is possibly more ignorant about many aspects of sexual behavior than many nonprofessionals. Indeed, it has been demonstrated that the average medical student and even the physician in practice tends to be no more knowledgeable or sexually experienced than his age peers in other branches of education, and that he may be less open than they in matters concerning sexual activity. Medicine attracts many controlled, highly moral young people so concerned with their work and with biological science that they have little time and energy left for the exploring and experimenting commonly undertaken by their contemporaries.

Few medical schools have offered a comprehensive course in human sexuality. Although it is customary to teach the anatomy and physiology of the reproductive system, little attention has been given to the peripheral physiology or psychosocial factors. Departments of urology and gynecology deal with some of the problems of somatic disease and departments of psychiatry with psychosexual development, but little consideration has been

8

given to the physiology of sexual intercourse and to the psychological and social aspects of sexual behavior. Sexual behavior
has only recently been described scientifically for the first time
in pioneering studies in the field. Today, however, many useful
books, including an AMA handbook, are available that elucidate the subject and may serve as guides for sexual and marital
counseling.

This report is designed to contribute to the physician's education in matters of sexual behavior, and particularly to help him
obtain appropriate sexual information from the patient in the
diversity of medical situations where it is relevant. We discuss
interviewing and describe representative situations in which
typical sexual problems appear. At the same time we review
the many types of sexual difficulty that are related to medical
problems in ways which may not always be immediately apparent. Thus we hope not only to help the physician but to
indicate how much more effectively he can offer treatment or
make appropriate referral when he is informed about the facts,
emotions and fantasies of his patient's sexual life.

The same principles of medical interviewing that apply elsewhere apply to the taking of a sexual history. Any interview is
a transaction between unique and complex individuals, and
should be conducted in a sensitive, nonmechanical way. System-
atic adherence to a predetermined outline will hardly elicit the
range and amount of information desired, yet a basic plan is
important and should be kept in mind if nothing of significance
is to be neglected. In general, the fewer direct questions the
better, and the fewer the questions to which the patient can
give a one-word reply, the more open the disclosure is likely to
be. Skill grows with practice.

The physician's attitude

The attitude and manner of the physician himself will largely
determine whether or not a meaningful and accurate picture
of the patient's sexual situation is obtained. Any anxiety or dis-

comfort the physician brings to such an interview will be communicated to the patient. This can seriously hamper the establishment of rapport and freedom of disclosure. The physician should take into account any of his own unresolved attitudes and conflicts, since these can impede his interaction with the patient and impair his understanding of the patient's situation.

For example, unsuccessfully resolved homosexual anxiety may make it difficult for the physician to frame questions on this subject, or to seek out information about oral or anal sexual activity. Or his failure to have worked through his own relationship to parent figures may pose problems for the physician who seeks sexual information from mature patients, especially patients much older than he. The physician who is convinced that the patient's sexual life is "none of his business" may be covering up unconscious anxieties and guilt feelings about his own sexual curiosity or may be allowing his guilty feelings about intrusion to inhibit his questioning. On the other hand, he may overcompensate for such feelings by overaggressive pursuit of a determined but insensitively dehumanized investigation.

It is a basic tenet of good interviewing that the physician refrain from imposing his own values on his patient. He should never allow value conflicts to compromise the conscientious execution of his professional responsibilities. Such restraint may be particularly difficult for a physician to exercise in taking a sexual history, but it is critical to the outcome of the interview. Attitudes toward sex vary widely according to the background and experience of the individual, and our rapidly changing contemporary cultural patterns reveal sharply disparate social sanctions. Thus the interviewer's personal code may well be at odds with his patient's.

The sensitive interviewer will be aware that his task is especially delicate where there is an ethnic, racial or social-class difference between himself and the interviewee. This difference suggests to him that they will have difficulty in understanding one another's language with reference to sexual activity or body parts, or in sharing a common view of the social values in which sex plays a part. He may try what he considers appropriate vernacular (i.e., saying *cock* for *penis*), but this is a superficial solution and one that may actually obstruct rapport by being interpreted as a demeaning condescension. A member of a minority group may find it difficult to speak openly about sexual behavior which he perceives as aberrant in the interviewer's culture. This uneasiness should be appreciated. The situation not only requires that the interviewer maintain a nonjudgmental stance, but that he convey the genuineness of his neutrality to his patient.

Another situation fraught with anxiety on both sides is the interview of a homosexual by a heterosexual. The ambivalence, defensiveness, and often judgmental attitude of the neophyte interviewing a homosexual frequently enhance the complex feelings of the patient, which may reflect the anxiety, shame and anger noted in many homosexuals when they deal with the "straight" world. A number of medical schools are finding that an effective way of desensitizing students to homosexuals is to invite representatives of the Gay Liberation movement or other homosexuals willing to discuss their life style to meet with groups of medical students.

When an interviewer feels anxiety and embarrassment in taking a sexual history he may be responding to the inhibiting effect of having grown up in an environment that proscribed specifically sexual conversation with anyone but intimates—if, indeed, it was tolerated at all. Or he may simply be suffering competence anxiety as he approaches an unfamiliar aspect of the otherwise familiar situation in which he is accustomed to mastery. He should not be too hard on himself if he evaluates his initial performance as poor. Many technical problems arise from inexperience in asking about sexual behavior, or from uncertainty about the purpose of such questioning.

Competence anxiety may reflect a lack of training or supervision. It can be overcome by increasingly familiarizing one-self with the rapidly expanding body of knowledge about the physiology and psychology of sex. It is true that in this highly charged kind of interview, unfortunate phraseology or the question that is too blunt may cause a patient to withdraw, but a single error, or indeed several errors, need not ruin the interview when the examiner is sensitive to the patient's response and is able to recognize and comment on his own "mistake" in a way that will promote trust and comfort. A relaxed matter-of-fact display of interest—without jocularity—is usually effective in all phases of the interview, but the specifics of the approach will depend on the interviewer's personality and on his interaction with the personality of each patient.

Direct supervision by an experienced interviewer who can offer a critique of one's skill can be helpful, and an opportunity to observe the experienced interviewer working with a patient is valuable. Often both aids can be utilized where a one-way mirror and audio equipment can be installed in the room assigned for the interview, or where a video recording can be made and played back later. The beginner should be selective in his learning, however, so that his own developing style will not be too imitative or become stilted or mechanical on this account.

The frequency with which sexual problems are identified in medical practice reflects the physician's initiative in seeking sexual information and his ease in discussing sexual material. Reports have shown that very little sexual disclosure is made by unselected patients when the physician conveys distaste for such discussion; frequency of disclosure rises when he asks questions about sex that are specifically indicated by the patient's situation; it rises significantly higher when sexual questions are routinely included in the interview by a physician who is himself undisturbed by their inclusion.

Any comprehensive patient work-up should contain at least enough of a sexual history to establish the patient's general attitude toward this aspect of life, and the relationship of his sexual activity to his age, occupation, social class, and other vital statistics. Sexual matters should be explored in depth whenever the initial interview suggests the possibility of problems and, in most cases, when a significant psychological component of the illness is suspected. An extensive investigation is obviously in order when sexual difficulty is the chief complaint. Clinical experience will alert the astute physician to the possibility that sexual or marital problems underlie such physical or psychic symptoms as headache, backache, fatigue, menstrual irregularities or dysmenorrhea and depression. Sexual dissatisfaction is a great imitator of many disease states.

One should recognize that undue curiosity lies at the other end of the spectrum from the notion that the patient's sexual life is "none of the doctor's business." This conflict motivates the physician who unnecessarily seeks descriptions of sexual episodes or whose overemphasis on the sexual history leaves a deficiency in a more general understanding of his patient's condition.

Seductive aspects of the interview

One cannot overlook the ever-present possibility that a patient will manifest certain attitudes and behaviors which can engage the physician in behavior he should be avoiding. A seductive female patient may evoke an overprotective response in the physician to the point where he teases her in a playful way; or a patient's extremely seductive conduct may evoke from the physician a cold and arrogant defense against such an erotic approach.

Unfortunately, physicians may have intercourse with their patients more often than is commonly recognized. The physician so involved often rationalizes his conduct by indicating that it is in the interest of the therapeutic requirements. Although it is usual for sexual feelings to be stirred up in the course of psychotherapy or sexual counseling, the engagement of a therapist in sexual interaction with a patient generally indicates that he is seeking an outlet for his own frustrations through such behavior or that he is using sexual behavior to meet his own needs for security and power, or to gain stature in his patient's eyes or in his own. Grandiose fantasies of freeing the patient from sexual inhibition by such behavior are hazardous to the therapist whose life situation is unstable, however one might interpret his professional ethics in such a situation.

There might be a certain logic in supposing that some patients could be helped by having intercourse with a sexually experienced partner in what might be considered a "therapeutic sexual relation," and it is possible that an occasional professional may engage in a sexual relationship with a patient for reasons other than the satisfaction of neurotic needs of his own such as those we have mentioned. However, we believe such a treatment approach contraindicated by the possibility of arousing in the patient unconscious incestuous feelings based on the strong identification (transference) that typically equates the clinician with the parent. If a therapeutic sexual relationship is indicated, the partner should be someone other than the clinician himself.

Confidentiality

The matter of confidentiality—and the patient's expectations on this score—must be taken into consideration. Most patients assume confidentiality as an aspect of the trust they place in their physician. Some, however, may ask for a special pledge of confidentiality. The interviewer should understand this special concern and offer quiet reassurance that any highly personal information is altogether secure with him. Information about a patient is ordinarily exchanged freely among the physicians involved in his care, but this practice may be inappropriate when applied to sexual information and must surely be restricted whenever an involved physician is close to the patient or his family. In such a situation, the physician anticipating his patient's anxiety might bring it out in the open: "Perhaps you are not being as frank with me as you would like to be

because you are afraid I might discuss your case with Dr. X."
In general, however, reassurance about the privileged nature of
the relationship is more sensitively conveyed by the physician's
manner than by any statements he might make.

The issue of confidentiality as applied to hospital records
poses a dilemma. We want to share as much information as
possible with all who are professionally concerned, but we must
be discreet about some personal matters and be on guard not to
reveal information about others who may be involved in the
patient's sexual behavior. Unfortunately, hospital records have
become more and more readily available to insurance com-
panies and social agencies, and may be subpoenaed in legal
action. Yet by careful wording one can often indicate for the
record general areas of sexual difficulty without giving damaging
details or implicating other identifiable persons. Nevertheless,
it is necessary for an understanding of the difficulties of some
patients that a highly specific record of sexual information be
made. Under some circumstances this record can be kept in a
coded file in the doctor's office apart from general hospital
records. Different hospitals and different physicians have different ways of handling this problem. It is enough here to point
out some of its ramifications and to emphasize the need for each
physician to find his own best solution.

Introductory interview sequences

The experienced physician not hampered by interfering personal conflicts can in most instances obtain quite a detailed
sexual history in his first interview with a patient. (As noted,
some general assessment of sexual functioning is indicated in
any comprehensive work-up. The extent will vary with the
problems encountered.) The subject is most appropriately
broached after enough time has been allowed for the establishment of rapport in other areas of inquiry. An opportunity to
explore the patient's sexual life may not appear spontaneously
in the interview, but there are a number of natural ways to in-

troduce the subject. Should the details of the present illness suggest a contributory sexual problem, inquiry may begin at this point. Or it may relate logically to a discussion of a woman's menses and her physical health; talk of the menarche and her attitude toward it can lead to confidences about the more personal aspects of her sexual life. Sexual information may be elicited from either men or women who are married in reference to the marriage and the marital partner.

Here direct questioning is usually not out of place. Where the direct question is inappropriate, the interviewer conveys by a calm, nonjudgmental attitude that there is very little which cannot be discussed, and he uses "bridges" to move the interview along. It is possible to move from the invitation "Tell me some of the good and bad things about your marriage" to "How does what you were just telling me affect your sexual relationship?" With the single woman one may move from the discussion of the menarche to a discussion of dating, petting, and any experience of intercourse she may have had. With a middle-class male patient one may go from wet dreams to masturbation or encounters with prostitutes or other sexual behaviors he may regard as shameful. Male patients from a social class not the interviewer's may require a different approach. The direction moves from less sensitive to more sensitive topics.

Often it is easier to uncover the patient's attitudes than to learn about his personal experiences. Indeed, attitudes may be more important than actual behavior. The physician may remark, "There are a lot of questions these days about oral-genital sex. How do you feel about it?" This approach is based on the principle that it is easier for a patient to talk about anything the physician suggests is universal, or at least common, than to talk about something that may be unusual or suspect. For example, the patient is more likely to reply negatively to the question "Did you ever masturbate?" but usually acknowledges the practice readily when asked "How young were you when you started to masturbate?" This approach unlocks the information when, how often, and with what fantasies and guilt the patient masturbates. However, a matter-of-fact attitude is not necessarily conveyed by abruptness or tactlessness. Through sensitivity and tact the physician transmits the feeling to his patient that there is very little about human life which cannot be discussed between them.

Another useful technique is to ascertain what expectations the patient had about certain experiences before actually undergoing them. After the first question, "What kind of sexual satisfaction did you expect when you got married?" the second follows easily: "How have your actual experiences matched your expectations?" This is another approach that generally unlocks the information sought.

Along with the physician's own style, the specific uses to which the inquiry is to be put will determine much of the conduct of any sexual history-taking. Is the questioning a prelude to treatment? Will the interviewing physician be treating the patient himself or make a referral? Is he going to present his report to a conference where there is a premium on comprehensive findings rather than on sensitivity to a patient's needs? In any case, throughout the interview the physician must be alert to the demands of the situation, and he should be supportive or objective as required. As the interview progresses, he must note any discomfort on the part of his patient, change the topic when necessary, and occasionally explain the reasons underlying a question. In short, he should display that overall demeanor of empathic objectivity appropriate for the professional face to face with a patient.

2

SEXUAL PROBLEMS OF THE MARITAL COUPLE

It seems appropriate here to consider first the married couple, or the couple living together in an informal sexual relationship important enough to involve the partners in a concern for its quality. With the understanding that marriage is the model in our culture and is central to our consideration of sexual behavior, we can deal under this subject heading with all couples who seek advice for problems in which sex plays a part.

The term *marital unit* is used by some to emphasize the concept that success or failure in sexual function depends on each of the partners and is a mutual responsibility. In viewing this sex-pair relationship it seems apparent also that compatibility between the partners in nonsexual aspects of their common life is intimately linked with their sexual communication.

It goes without saying that love is a major ingredient of all but the most passing of sexual relationships. The quality and intensity of love will be important to assess. Because the word *love* covers such complex multifaceted dimensions of human relationships, we will not discuss it as such to any great extent in this book. We do emphasize that sexuality is only one dimension of human life and loving and that it should be evaluated in the context of the patient's total life situation.

Occasionally a couple struggling with what they think of as a sexual problem will consult a physician together. More frequently a sexual difficulty will be uncovered by the physician's care in interviewing the patient who comes ostensibly, or real-

istically, with another complaint. When one partner discloses
a sexual problem, it is usually important that the physician see
the other as well—a conjoint interview is almost always indicated. Some physicians prefer to see the partners together at the
outset, with individual interviews to follow. Others prefer to
begin with individual interviews and then go on to a conjoint
session.

There are many advantages in interviewing husband and wife
together and being able to observe their interaction at first hand.
The way they look at one another and talk together reveals
something of their feelings and attitudes. Bodily movements,
facial expressions, and other nonverbal communications may
convey concern, protective sympathy, disdain or anger. It is
possible to see how each partner controls power in the relationship and uses or abuses it. Where a wife complains of her husband's failure to show affection, one may directly appraise his
capacity to feel and to express emotion. By seeing both partners
together the physician is in a position to sense the range of sensitivity, emotional response, expressiveness and awareness of
which each is capable.

Every marital situation is a complex multidimensional system based on the way in which each partner sees the other and
sees the marriage itself, on the self-image of each, and on each
partner's perception of how he or she appears to the other. The
physician can check this interlocking system in a conjoint interview and obtain immediate feedback. After the wife has
answered the question, "How do you think your husband feels
about the way you respond to him in bed?" the interviewer can
turn to the husband to ask, "How does this fit in with the way
you feel about her sexual response?" Such inquiry will not only
lay bare the framework of the marriage, but will also reveal the
ability of each partner to communicate. Often it is helpful to
have one spouse repeat what the other has said, to insure that
one of them is not being "tuned out" by the other. Even the
evaluating interview can be therapeutic when it improves by
such means the communication between man and wife.

Masters and Johnson pioneered a special type of conjoint interview and therapy in which each partner is initially interviewed by a therapist of the same sex before being seen by a therapist of the opposite sex; both partners and both interviewers then go into conjoint meeting. The assumption is that one person can disclose some matters more readily to a member of the same sex and another to a member of the opposite sex.

Among other advantages of the Masters and Johnson conjoint interview, which merits wider use, is the likelihood that when two interviewers each of a different sex are present, the development of conflictual transference relationships is minimized. This conjoint technique also tends to inhibit the wife from behaving seductively toward a male therapist and further estranging her husband.

Types of sexual problems

One complaint masks another. Even when the partners recognize their sexual difficulty it may not be the complaint they present to the physician. Some other aspects of marital discord may be stressed, as in the following:

> CASE EXAMPLE 1: A 29-year-old woman, the wife of a physician recently established in practice, sought help ostensibly because of incompatibility of their religious and humanistic values. She complained bitterly about her husband's excessively competitive, pushy attitude and his lack of interest in causes she considered deserving of his support.
>
> *Only in response to direct questions did she reveal that she had never experienced orgasm during her marriage.* Upon reaching a certain stage of sexual excitment she would do anything to end the stimulation in order to avoid heightening the excitment. She was so afraid of orgasm that she was reluctant even to discuss this aspect of her marital adjustment.

Other patients, aware of their sexual problems and anxious to discuss them, may be too reticent to initiate discussion unless the interviewer broaches the subject. They complain of other difficulties, which may be genuine enough:

> CASE EXAMPLE 2: A young married woman sought medical care because of headaches and painful spasms of neck and back muscles. In the course of the interview the physician began to suspect underlying emotional difficulties. A tactful inquiry about her marriage evoked expressions of resentment toward her husband.
>
> *This had to do with the fact that she was being pressured to have oral-genital contact, which she resisted. She was convinced that her husband was a pervert* and that the physician would be shocked by this disclosure. However, as his equanimity and interest encouraged her to go on talking, she was able to overcome her embarrassment and to express her concern about this matter, which had caused frequent arguments and which lay behind her somatic complaints.

Complaints recognized by the sufferer to be sexual may be grouped into (1) those openly named as the chief complaint, (2) those borne in silence despite significant discomfort and considerable preoccupation with them, and (3) problems of dysfunction the significance of which is denied by the patient, who stresses other areas of marital discord in an effort to avoid any change in sexual adjustment or any scrutiny of the crucial issue.

Although sexuality is integral to the total relationship of two sexual partners, sexual problems may be thought of as either primary or secondary. Primary sexual problems may be defined as those in which the basic issue is clearly sexual and is of sufficient magnitude to cause severe marital incompatibility. These sexual problems typically have existed for one or both of the partners since the beginning of the marriage and often antedate it. Secondary sexual problems may be defined as those rooted in other difficulties besetting the marital relationship;

they usually appear in the course of a marriage the sexual life of which has been fairly satisfactory until damaged by resentment, anxiety or guilt arising from conflict in another area.

Although the classifications used by marital counseling agencies tend to be far from precise, it has been estimated that about 75 per cent of the couples who seek counseling at such agencies have significant sexual problems, and four out of five in this group have sexual problems of a secondary nature.

Problems of ignorance. Primary sexual problems often stem from ignorance, or from faulty learning or conditioning. Ignorance about sex often indicates the inhibiting effect on learning of anxiety and guilt. The physician will want to ascertain the extent of each partner's knowledge about sex, the congruence of their attitudes about it, and the degree to which one partner communicates with the other about it. It is necessary to assess the patient's knowledge of his or her own sexual physiology, and that of the partner, as well as the expectations each of them has of the sexual relationship. The shame or fear of rejection that society engenders in so many of its members often inhibits discussion about sex to the point that communication on the subject between partners is virtually nonexistent.

Nevertheless many people worry privately about how frequently coitus should take place, whether oral-genital contact is a perversion, what the coital position should be, and how long intercourse should last. One or both of the partners may have unrealistic expectations of what the other expects or what the other should be able to give. The woman who expects orgasm in each act of coitus, or, having heard about multiple orgasms, feels inadequate if she has only one, provides a good example of such unrealistic expectations. Or a couple may feel dissatisfaction when they fail to have simultaneous orgasm with each union. Or the man may consider himself impotent if he cannot have three or four ejaculations a night. Frequently the way in which a partner initiates sexual activity creates problems. The husband or wife who expects the spouse to welcome sex on demand, who understands nothing of the ways in which stimulation affects mood and desire, may in reality be responding to the partner's inability to discuss such aspects of sexuality.

It is important for the physician to know that sexual difficulties can exist in the absence of significant psychopathology. It is often possible to give real help—and sometimes to solve the problem—by taking simple steps toward clarification and education, and by reassuring the couple that certain attitudes and behavior patterns are normal. It is just as often possible to be therapeutically effective by facilitating a new level of communication between the partners.

Problems secondary to other aspects of the joint life. The physician will want to assess the life style and past sexual experience of each partner, as well as any differences in religious, social or ethical background, since he will be working toward general conclusions about the nature of the marital interaction. He will be interested in the quality of the affiliative forces at work (love, tenderness, mutual respect) and in the existence of any conflict that could engender hostility, disrespect or anxiety. Often he learns that one or each of the partners feels that the other is not loving, which may or may not militate against adequate sexual performance. The next question to decide is whether the sexual situation has always been deficient or whether it has deteriorated during the marriage. In the first instance, the deficiency is probably related to personality characteristics of one spouse, as in the case of an obsessive or a schizoid individual who has great difficulty in expressing any tenderness.

CASE EXAMPLE 3: A woman consulted a marriage counselor because she felt unresponsive toward her husband but was becoming more and more "turned on" by a male friend, although she had not yet had any direct sexual contact with him. She was frightened by the temptation to have an affair with her friend and wondered if she could develop some of the same feelings toward her husband, a successful busi-

nessman and community leader for whom she had great
respect. He made love in an almost unvar\ing pattern,
routinely and mechanically. When interviewed he expressed great astonishment at his wife's lack of response, for
she had simulated orgasm throughout 20 years of married
life. He was a methodical, self-contained, unemotional man
who found it difficult to express affection. Many years of
sexual unhappiness could have been avoided had his wife
expressed her dissatisfaction earlier. She had been afraid
to do so lest she offend her husband so deeply that he would
leave her.

When a marriage that has been truly affectionate at the start
presents problems, they can usually be ascribed to the marital
interaction rather than to any specific personality difficulty. The
physician will focus on when and how the relationship changed,
and will look for such reasons as boredom or the development of
divergent interests. The complaint of one partner that the other
shows little affection must be carefully evaluated. Many individuals have such an exaggerated need for love and reassurance
that they find normal devotion inadequate.

Sexual dysfunction that appears in the course of a marriage is
often caused by an excess of anxiety, anger or guilt, and the interviewer will find such emotion in his patient a useful clue to the
underlying problem. Such negative emotions often awaken de-
fensive reactions aimed at reducing anxiety, protecting self-
esteem, or revenging oneself on the partner. For example, the
performance anxiety that leads to a man's impotence or premature ejaculation or unconscious hostility toward women may
have the same effect on sexual performance. Specifically, performance anxiety may arise from job stress, may be translated
into anxiety about sexual capability, and may then be further
compounded by sexual failure. A woman's motive in withhold-
ing enthusiastic sexual response may reflect her fear of becoming too dependent on her mate and too vulnerable to possible
future rejection; or she may be entirely absorbed by her new

role as a mother or may fear becoming pregnant. The loss of a loved one—or, more subtly, the loss of self-esteem—may create an underlying depression that reduces interest in sexuality. A rejected partner may become angry and either avoid the mate or make excessive demands, creating a vicious circle of dissatisfaction. It is not enough to identify the sexual problem—the physician will want to search among many possibilities for its cause.

Specific overt sexual dysfunction

The two most common reasons for a man to seek sexual counsel are premature ejaculation and impotence, two not dissimilar problems that may exist at different times in the same man.

Premature ejaculation. No precise definition of this term is available. It is clear enough that the man who ejaculates immediately upon entry ejaculates prematurely, but after recognizing this, how do we measure the timing of normal or premature performance? A pragmatic definition that seems appropriate as long as one is dealing with a stable marital unit is that ejaculation is premature when the male partner is able less than half the time to maintain coital contact long enough to make climax possible for a potentially fully responsive partner. The onus for premature ejaculation is generally placed on the male partner, but we have become aware of the repressive and negatively conditioning effect of our society on female sexuality and therefore should consider the possibility that the female partner is contributing to the problem by being very slow to achieve orgasm. Clearly we need more information about this complex phenomenon.

Although premature ejaculation is often caused by severe neurotic conflict, it could be the result of early conditioning to feelings of haste, excitement and fear that may have accompanied adolescent experimentation. The physician will want to find out exactly what is happening—whether ejaculation occurs before or after intromission, and how soon before or after. If ejaculation is not always premature, under what circumstances does it occur prematurely?

The reactions of a wife to this problem are important in assessing the prognosis and the type of therapy required. Her cooperation, added to the physician's counsel, can often alleviate the partner's performance anxiety.

> CASE EXAMPLE 4: A married man had been troubled by premature ejaculation since his first coital experience, which occurred before marriage. Afraid of failure, and anxious lest he displease his wife and lose his masculine pride, he found that the only way he could control his ejaculation was to turn off his erotic feelings altogether, except for the final moments of orgasm and ejaculation. He would concentrate on objects in the room, think of his business concerns—anything but the signals from his own body. This worked effectively until it became more and more difficult to become sufficiently aroused to attain an erection. Finally, impotence became his problem as well as his wife's. During treatment, in which he learned to experience erotic arousal even from rubbing his wife's hands, he mourned the loss of twenty years of sexual pleasure.

Impotence. When impotence is the chief problem, the physician must establish whether it always existed as a primary disability—that is, the individual may never have been potent with a woman—or whether it has developed secondarily—after previous demonstrated potency; and whether it characterizes the patient's experience with all women or only with certain partners. The so-called primarily impotent man is rare. When the history shows that the patient has never been able to achieve and maintain an erection and has never had a successful coital experience, it is clear that a severe and deeply rooted problem exists which should be referred to a skilled psychiatrist with special training, or to a marriage counselor with experience in treating such difficulties.

When the problem is one of secondary impotence, it is important to be meticulous in taking the history, and to bear in mind that a metabolic or structural impairment may be responsible. For example, diabetes is the most common non-psychogenic cause of secondary impotence. The history can be organized around the following:

1. *Circumstances in which secondary impotence first occurred.*—The first episode often occurs after excessive use of alcohol; or coitus is attempted when the man is extremely tired, worried, or distracted by interruptions (children's voices, unexpected phone calls). Other causes of the first failure may be anger toward the wife, her failure to respond, or guilty feelings toward her because of some real or fantasied unfaithfulness.

Occasionally the first episode is precipitated by an experience having no direct connection with the patient's sexual life—some failure at work, in school or social life, or some humiliation experienced outside the home.

The interview should be directed toward a precise determination of the circumstances surrounding the first episode.

2. *Patient's reaction to the symptom.*—The degree of embarrassment caused by this symptom varies. Some men feel so intensely about it that their entire life is affected, even to the point of serious depression and an inability to carry on. Usually the man redoubles his efforts to perform the sex act properly, and this effort compounds the problem, since he cannot will an erection any more than he can control his breathing for any length of time. The more he concentrates on performance, the less likely he is to have an erection or to maintain it when he does. Another common response is to shun sexual encounters in order to avoid embarrassment.

3. *Wife's reaction to the symptom.*—Sometimes the wife is understanding, sympathetic and supportive. Such an attitude makes treatment much easier. However, she is often

frustrated and angry and may increase her demands on her husband, perhaps seeking reassurance that she is not losing her attractiveness. Or she may withdraw from sexual activity to avoid frustration or spare her husband embarrassment. Any expression of disappointment or frustration on her part can only add to his humiliation.

4. *Nature of the marital interaction, including the sexual relationship.*—In most cases, secondary impotence is a response to other difficulties in the marriage. Interviewing should aim to elucidate the conflicts within the marriage as well as the affiliative forces that might improve the prognosis. A detailed account of the couple's previous sexual interaction will help to put the present problem in its historical context. One important factor is the wife's responsiveness; another is whether or not premature ejaculation preceded impotence.*

5. *Situational impotence.*—It is possible that a man impotent with his wife will be fully potent with a mistress, or the reverse may be true. Moreover, a man may be only occasionally impotent. It is important to discern the pattern of such variable performance, which may be based on the nature of the marital interaction and whether the wife is sexually responsive, sympathetic and supportive, or is antagonistic. A fairly representative example follows:

CASE EXAMPLE 5: A middle-aged engineer had been suffering from secondary impotence for two years. At the suggestion of their family physician, he and his wife saw a consultant together. She was a very responsive, warm and affectionate woman whose good-natured friendliness covered a great deal of anger toward her husband. However, she was eager to help. Seemingly, no definite precipitating factors had preceded her husband's impotence, and it was only when the therapist had won his trust and interviewed him alone that the man unburdened himself, confessing

---

* For a discussion of areas to cover in this review of marital interaction, see Masters and Johnson, HUMAN SEXUAL INADEQUACY, pp 34-51 (No. 22 in the Bibliography of this report, page 848).

that the impotence had immediately followed two unsuccessful attempts to have intercourse with another woman. Since his motivation for this extramarital encounter had been to be "one of the boys" with business colleagues who bragged about their conquests, and since he was in love with his wife, the relief of confessing his guilt quickly led to his becoming potent again.

Orgasmic dysfunction or frigidity. When the chief complaint is a woman's inability to obtain orgasm, inquiry is directed toward whether she has ever achieved one by any means, including masturbation. If she has never experienced orgasm, this is a problem she brought to the marriage; it generally indicates a major rejection of one's sexuality, based in early rearing and development. The physician seeks a thorough knowledge of the patient's childhood experience and an understanding of her relationships with parents and others. In most cases this condition (primary orgasmic dysfunction) will require referral to a specialist, who may be a psychiatrist with special experience in this area, a specially qualified clinical psychologist, or a marital counselor.

If the woman has experienced orgasm in the past, the occasions on which it was achieved will require investigation. Among the likely possibilities are self-masturbation, early mutual masturbation with another, or the mate's manual or oral manipulation. Some women will be able to achieve orgasm by the latter means but not in intercourse. If she was fully responsive during any period of her marriage, it is important to secure particulars about the onset of the symptom and her reaction to it. In the case of a woman who is orgastic in masturbation but is unable to achieve climax in marital sexual intercourse, the therapist must decide whether the problem is deeply inherent in the woman herself, or whether it is a more superficial inhibition arising out of her husband's lack of understanding or failure to communicate.

A failure to respond to sexual intercourse with orgasm, when not due to ignorance, often is due to the inhibiting effects of any of a variety of emotions. Guilt, anger and fear are frequently involved. The woman may have such guilty feelings about the full enjoyment of sexual pleasure that she unconsciously rejects it. The fear of pregnancy, too, must always be considered as a possible determinant.

Infidelity

Whenever the sexual compatibility of a reasonably good marriage has been abruptly impaired, the possibility of infidelity must be considered by the physician. Inquiry about a possible extramarital relationship should be made of one partner in the absence of the other unless the existence of such an entanglement is already known to both, in which event it may be openly discussed. It is amazing how often a couple will refrain, by a kind of tacit collusion, from discussing an extramarital affair which is far from being a secret. Bringing the situation into the open may actually improve the relationship between the marriage partners. This situation challenges the skillful physician with the possibility of serving his patients by opening up appropriate channels of communication between them.

A tactful approach to the possibility of infidelity may be in order: "To what extent have you been attracted to or involved with someone besides your spouse?" If there has been extramarital involvement, the physician should ascertain whether or not it is known to the mate, and what reasons lie behind it. He can then decide how to handle the information he has elicited, against the background of the moral, religious, and other attitudinal sets of each partner.

Homosexuality and bisexuality in the marital situation

It may be difficult to probe the marriage threatened by homosexual impulses or behavior by one or both of the partners, especially when shame or secrecy beclouds the issue. Combining the historical approach with the technique of "ubiquity," the physician can proceed quickly to a leading question: "About a third of all men have had homosexual contact to the point of orgasm during their adolescence, and the experience of women, though somewhat less widespread, is similar. What has been your experience?" Affirmative information may be followed by questions phrased to elicit the fact of any repeated homosexual encounters, trouble with homosexual fantasies, or fears of being homosexual. This line of inquiry is important because many of the most stubborn cases of heterosexual dysfunction have been shown to arise from latent homosexual fantasies and impulses, or from the sufferer's fear that he or she is homosexual. Even where such fear is clearly unjustified, as is usually the case, doubts about one's masculinity or femininity can contribute to the development of a sexual problem.

3

ASSESSING SEXUAL FUNCTIONING OF CHILDREN

Familiarity with the range of physical, emotional and cognitive development that may be expected at any given chronological age is helpful in securing sexual information about or from a child. The patient should be perceived as an incomplete and still evolving human being, one with a future as well as a past. Familiarity with the interrelated developmental sequences of childhood will help the physician understand how the child's current status will affect his later development and, conversely, how his unfolding future will affect the current situation. The interplay of environmental factors also deserves careful consideration.

Since the physician is usually in touch with parents or other caretakers of his young patient, he can often assess environmental pressures being brought to bear on the child. The very young child can contribute little or no background information in his own behalf, so that the physician must depend on the statements of involved adults, the reliability of which may be open to question. How often has a parent assured the pediatrician that the child "never plays with himself," while the child is in fact masturbating right before their eyes.

Even when suffering, a child is unlikely to follow the adult pattern of trying to get help by cooperating in the history-taking, a process which for this reason will require the physician's special consideration. Although he often faces the adult patient with the gravest problem at the outset of an interview,

such directness when dealing with a child could handicap the
establishment of rapport or even destroy it. Rather the interviewer should proceed by indirection, talking about the child's
own interests before turning to the problem. He must nevertheless take pains not to seem deceitful. Children often encounter
duplicity in adults, and experience leads them to anticipate
deceit on the part of the physician, especially when he puzzles
them by a friendly, humane, unaccusing manner in the face of
what they know is the purpose of the interview. It is all too easy
in dealing with children to assume thoughtlessly an attitude
which the child can interpret as bad faith. A suspicious child is
not likely to put his fears into words, but nonverbal clues will
betray his anxiety. The interviewer may have to rely on intui-
tion to alert him to the right time for bringing his motives and
honest intention out into the open; at such times an exchange
will clear the air and facilitate the obtaining of a sexual history.

The style of the interview will depend on the purpose of the
history-taking, the interviewer's role, how well he knows the
child, and the developmental stage of the child, since different
sexual issues emerge at different levels of maturity. With a pre-
school child it might be natural and informative during the
examination to ask him to name the parts of his body and
perhaps indicate their function. Children this young are often
concerned about differences between the sexes and about theories of reproduction Older children may be more concerned
with masturbation and sexual play. Somewhat later, the issue
of modesty in the home or in school becomes important. Sleep-
ing, toileting and bathing arrangements in the home may concern a child throughout his development.

Communicating with young children

The following gives an example of useful communication with
a 4-year-old:

> CASE EXAMPLE 6: A 4-year-old girl's parents were con-
> cerned about her jealousy of a sister younger by 15 months.

During a psychiatric evaluation, Ellen expressed interest in having a baby of her own. The doctor explored with her the question of whether the baby her mother would carry would be Ellen's or her mother's. Ellen indicated her realization that she would have to wait until she could have her own baby inside of her. She claimed that her mother had promised her a baby brother, but in a subsequent interview retracted this. She and her sister had both "come out girls," but she wanted a boy. In response to the doctor's inquiry about where she thought babies come from, she at first asserted that her mother went to the hospital and got the baby there.

Later she added that the mother carries the baby inside and "gets all puffed up." In reply to the doctor's questions, she made it clear that she knew girls could do this but boys couldn't. The doctor then asked about other differences between boys and girls, and Ellen blurted out that boys have a penis and girls don't, looking sad as she remarked that this was an awfully good thing for boys. When the doctor asked if there was anything girls had or could do that boys couldn't, she said that girls have "fannies." She seemed proud of that, and added that girls can make wee-wee through their fannies, but boys can't. The doctor asked her to tell him other good things about girls, and Ellen became quite enthusiastic when her thoughts returned to the fact that girls could have babies. As she talked about having to wait, her mood returned to one of sadness and she said she only could wait "two days," but that she would *have* to wait hundreds and hundreds of days. She concluded that she *thought* she would be able to do that.

The doctor sought other information about Ellen's psychosexual development and interests, determining that she derived pleasure from walking around naked in her home and that she was unwilling to make sure always that the wee-wee went into the toilet. She communicated mixed pleasure and anxiety in talking about mud pies and playing in mud puddles.

Without knowing the contents of the interview, Ellen's

mother reported that she seemed more open and communi-
cative at home after these two psychiatric assessments,
which had led the doctor to the conclusion that Ellen was a
psychologically normal 4-year-old.

When the interviewer is a physician and no physical examination is planned, the child's anxiety about a physical examination, possible injections and the like should be allayed,
while the physician's novel role can be explained as his wish to
become acquainted with the child and his thinking and feelings.
The use of toys. Toys can be used to facilitate communication
between the interviewer and young children, who often find it
easier to communicate their interests and concerns by dis-
placing them onto dolls, puppets or other toys. Through such
play they are likely to express personally relevant feelings, so
that it is entirely appropriate to talk with a child seriously
about the doll's experiences, feelings, interests and concerns.
Although much can be learned through a free, unstructured
play situation, such play may be structured in advance when it
is necessary to communicate with the very young child about a
specific and possibly traumatic experience.

For example, if the issue is the enticement of a very young
child into sexual activity with an adult who offered candy as a
lure, the interviewer might set up a situation in which dolls
represent the persons involved in the episode. He tells the child
that the adult doll has just offered candy to the child doll. He
should bear in mind, of course, that the activity is designed to
facilitate communication with the youngster and is not aimed at
extracting a confession.

Direct verbalization may be preferable in seeking information about a similar situation from an older child. Here the
interviewer might modify the technique of "ubiquity" as follows: "Mother and Dad told me that you got mixed up with
this older person. Other kids have found it worthwhile to tell
me what happened and how they felt. . . ."

Semantics. Not only should the interviewer of children understand the importance of nonverbal communication from the
younger child, but he should also be aware of the different mean-
ings words and phrases hold for children at different stages of
their development. There are other semantic traps as well. The
word *feel* is often used in interviewing, for example, and
although it may represent an emotional abstraction to the interviewer, the immature patient may think of it only in the sense
of *touch*. Words like *queer, cool* and—significantly—*why* may
have different connotations for different age groups.

Surprising reactions are often elicited from the child asked
why he did or said something. Even when his capacity for abstraction allows him to appreciate the interviewer's real interest
in determining a causal relationship, he may consider "Because"
an adequate reply, a reply at the same time reflecting his
feeling of being under criticism. It is likely that this reflects
past occasions when an adult *why* was less a question than an
agonized warning to the offender not to repeat whatever sin he
had just committed. Any reader interested in confirming this
observation might examine his own queries to his own children
and see how seldom he asks *why* about actions or thoughts of
which he approves, and how frequently the word implies disapproval. We seldom question a child's motive in achieving anything worthwhile. We are ready enough to ask *why* a school
failure has occurred, but unlikely to question the motivation
behind an all-A report card. The message the interviewer sends
is not always the message the child receives when we interrogate
him. Although ambiguity should be avoided to the extent
possible, it is almost inevitably present. It therefore behooves
the interviewer to take this into account and to deal with it in a
way that will be helpful to his young patient.

Communicating with older children

When the older child comes to his physician with a physical
complaint such as a fracture, appendicitis, an eye disease, or

whatever, a sexual history may be noncontributory to the matter at hand. However, the patient-physician encounters that do take place at a time when the older child's defenses are apt to be down and his cooperation is forthcoming give the physician an opportunity to identify himself as a helpful and trustworthy counselor to whom sexual perplexities and problems may be brought as the child matures. If it is considered wise to take a sexual history in the interest of completeness and for good medical practice, the treatment of the physical illness with little or no sexual involvement may permit the introduction of sexual issues in an offhand manner. Often the physician can simply say that he is exploring this area in the interest of completeness and in order to know the youngster as well as he can. The physician's care *not* to be aggressive will promote rapport, but the subject may be introduced directly:

> We've talked about a lot of things in your life but very little about your dating experience and general sexual adjustment. This is an important part of anyone's life, and during the teen years everybody seems to have some frustrations and conflicts about it, so it might be a good idea to talk about it now.

A youngster too proud to acknowledge discomfort, conflicts or inhibitions may appreciate a chance to talk about the hangups of his friends as a preliminary to exploring his own. The young male physician should realize that the young girl he interviews about her sexuality may be shy and embarrassed—as he may very well be, himself—and that a professional and understanding but not seductive manner will make matters easier.

The question of sharing information with the parents, and of interpreting the information they supply, is an important one. Children usually find it easier to communicate with the physician who, they feel, will respect their confidences and will not relay the information they give him to anyone, including the parents, without their permission. It is usual to deal with parents before interviewing their children, but as the youngster approaches adolescence the physician should consider seeing him first, reserving for a later date his contact with the parents, based on the establishment of an understanding between himself and his patient.

4

INTERVIEWING ADOLESCENTS AND OTHER SINGLE PERSONS

Special considerations are involved in taking the sexual history of an unmarried person. Some of these reflect the disparity between the new life styles that have emerged in American society, and the physician's value system. Others require sensitivity to the true nature of fears and anxieties that lie beneath rationalized explanations of behavior. Still others pertain to the possibility that premarital counseling may be the purpose of the interview. And in many instances the turbulence of adolescence will complicate the picture.

Adolescents

Sexual issues are of such importance during adolescence that a sexual interview with an adolescent calls for sensitive attention to a variety of factors in the individual youngster's specific situation, as well as a knowledge of the psychodynamics of this period of life. It is naive to expect the adolescent patient to be reasonable, open and cooperative during a period in which he is undergoing rapid and apparently unpredictable mental and physical changes. These changes require him to distance himself from his parents and all the other adults he associates with them. Moreover, he must justify or rationalize behavior prompted by his search for identity, his fear of his own drive toward independence, his fear of sexual impulses toward his parents, and the threat of engulfment he senses in being close to a strong adult. A view of the adult (physician) as untrustworthy allows him to justify his discomfort on the ground that he is being victimized by someone hostile and treacherous.

For these reasons cooperation cannot be assumed even when serious illness necessitates the youngster's dependence on his physician. Thus any discussion of confidentiality must convey strong reassurance to the adolescent patient. It is often wise to say something like the following:

> You've probably had experience with adults who told you you could trust them but who let you down. I don't see why you should expect a stranger like me to be different, but if we keep on seeing one another the chances are that you'll find out whether or not I violate your trust and talk to your parents or other people about things you wouldn't want me to. So it might take a while for you to find out if you can really trust me.

The reasons for any adolescent's involvement with a physician —the type of illness, the kind of physician being seen, etc.— markedly affect the technique selected in approaching the sexual history. Some complaints are clearly sex-related: out-of-wedlock pregnancy, active sexuality that has attracted attention and disapproval, homosexuality, exhibitionism, and so on. Since the adolescent is fully aware of the reasons why he is being taken to a physician, a direct approach to the subject is advisable. Any indirection or pussyfooting not only invites negative interpretation but throws up a barrier between patient and physician at the outset.

The practical aspects of such problems often necessitate some sharing of confidential information, so that it is a good idea for the physician to indicate to his young patient at the beginning the ways in which confidentiality may of necessity be compromised at a later date. For example, adolescents are unlikely to object strenuously to the obviously real need in certain cases to make at least minimal reports to a court, or to object where the physician must discuss with the parents issues with which they are already concerned. What does offend and alienate the adolescent is the failure to show enough respect for him to tell him about these limitations of confidentiality in the first place.

When the requirements of disclosure cannot be determined in advance—and, indeed, no one can anticipate what the patient will reveal to him—the physician may suggest that his young patient stipulate precisely those events or issues he wants kept secret. He agrees to keep them secret, then, unless it becomes necessary to disclose them in the youngster's best interests, at which time the youngster's permission to do so will be sought and his views discussed. This arrangement may be qualified openly by the physician's warning that in the event of disagreement between them about disclosure, the physician's judgment must prevail. At the same time the physician should state plainly that if the patient should later prove to be unavailable in an emergency, the physician's best judgment would here again prevail. Although such an approach may seem elaborate, adolescents usually find such straightforwardness acceptable, and care given to this point is often justified by the health-threatening and even life-threatening situations that can arise in treatment of an adolescent and that often demand disclosure of confidential information.

Where the chief complaint is probably sex-related but the relationship is obscure or undisclosed, a sexual history is necessary, but it may be advisable to postpone taking it until the patient has had a chance to air all his conscious concerns and thoughts about his difficulty. Generalized anxiety, depression, moodiness, poor school performance, acne, or vague somatic complaints with no organic cause could be related to guilt about masturbation, sexual wishes, fantasies or activities, or to anxiety over pubescent and adolescent body changes. The doctor may suggest that the complaints made are of a kind often related to guilt or anxiety, and offer a few simple examples to illustrate the possibility. The discussion of sexuality that follows should parallel that already suggested for the patient with directly sex-related problems, except that it will have taken place after a lengthier preliminary exchange.

The patient who uses drugs, who is a runaway, or who is schizophrenic may have sexual problems as a component of more comprehensive emotional difficulty. Some youngsters in this category have only the most tenuous and reluctant ties with the adult world. Any inquiry which they interpret as irrelevant or prying can make them bolt and thus preclude the physician's usefulness. Some adolescents may have ego strength so fragile that premature questioning about sexuality could disorganize them; it is therefore often wise to wait until the external, realistic situation has stabilized and rapport has been established before exploring an area as personal as sexuality.

The physician faced with the task of helping a young person whose life style and appearance offend him will be making a mistake if he prejudges his patient on the basis of a superficial impression. First of all, an account of unorthodox behavior is not, *per se,* evidence of psychopathology. Actually we know very little as yet about the incidence of psychopathology among those who adopt the life styles of the "sexual revolution." Second, a "liberated" appearance and manner may be bravely adopted by a youngster who is in reality anxious, inexperienced, and pretty much of an imposter in any one of a number of ways. The boy with long hair and love beads may be terrified of sex, and may lack any sexual experience. The girl who flamboyantly displays her physical endowment may be chaste and determined to stay that way. On the other hand, the mousy young woman with the earnest look may be very active sexually. Social class, ethnic and religious background, and locale enter into the way young people present themselves. Evidence of the youth rebellion may have determinants other than the rebellion itself.

Puritanical stances. On occasion the physician will find that what his outwardly peer-conforming young patient actually wants from him is his support in continuing to adhere to a staunchly defended inner value system that has caused conflict with his peers.

> CASE EXAMPLE 7: An 18-year-old freshman at a coeducational college consulted her physician because of marked anxiety, depression, and inability to concentrate on her studies. She was determined to be a virgin until she married. Her value system had been inculcated by her parents and she had firmly adopted it. She was exposed to considerable stress in school on two counts: She frequently felt sexual arousal while dating, and she was confronted by intense group pressure to engage in premarital intercourse, being subjected to considerable ridicule for her resistance.
> Dependent on her peers for approval, she was in such turmoil that she sought professional help. It was necessary for the physician to support her autonomous position while she sought out new friends who shared her value system.

The young patient who takes pride in adhering to old-fashioned sexual morality may need another kind of help, since his morality may not represent a free and thoughtful choice, but rather indicate fear. The physician who can help his patient deal with such fear may prevent lifelong emotional crippling. There is the fear of being psychologically and physically intimate with anyone; the fear of marriage as a trap; performance anxiety; fear of pregnancy; fear of the sex act as an act of violence; and fear arising from a sense of moral guilt.

The fear of intimacy often accounts for avoidance of sexual closeness. Intimacy is a congruent fusion of sexuality and closeness in which the closeness does not strangle, but permits an appropriate resumption of independence in the satisfaction of individual needs and wishes. It includes the sharing of pain as well as the sharing of pleasure, and depends on the individual's capacity to unite with another. Some people fear that such union would make them vulnerable. They resist becoming dependent on anyone else for a necessary pleasure. Others fear the loss of control implicit in the experience of orgasm.

Promiscuity. The other side of the coin is promiscuity, often caused by an ever-unsatisfied search for intimacy that sends the youngster expectantly from one experience to another in a succession of sexual encounters which promise closeness but almost invariably disappoint.

The meaning of marriage. Some people are afraid of marriage itself, rationalizing their feeling logically enough on the high divorce rate and the apparent incompatibility of the marriages they see around them. Short-term fidelity has a higher value for many young people than any promise of permanence. They hesitate to enter into an arrangement which seems to them to offer as little promise of success as does marriage. Some are so afraid of being caught in a situation with no escape hatch or of making a bad mistake in choosing a mate that they avoid sexual experience or engage in it only with great anxiety.

Performance anxiety. Performance anxiety has been discussed in the preceding section, and the way in which early conditioning carries over into later life has been indicated. Early experience of performance anxiety, followed by premature ejaculation, impotence, or failure to reach orgasm, followed in turn by increased fear, more marked incapacity, or greater tension, establishes the basis for later difficulty. The physician will bring to his interviews with the single patient on this subject many of the insights he uses in counseling the married person with a like problem.

The fear of pregnancy. The fear of pregnancy leads many young unmarried girls to consult a physician for contraceptive advice and materials, and such requests can put him into a most uncomfortable position. He should, however, remind himself that the girl's decision to engage in premarital intercourse and her decision to use a contraceptive are separate issues, and that his advice is being specifically sought on the second issue only. It has been unusual for an unmarried girl to ask professional advice about whether or not to have intercourse. Any value conflicts she may have about this are usually displaced onto a concern about contraception or to other aspects of an admitted relationship, masked by feelings of anxiety or depression, or expressed by physical symptoms. The physician makes his decision, then, after weighing the relative harm of (1) failing to prevent an unwanted pregnancy and (2) giving tacit consent to premarital intercourse by providing contraception. The latter course is now favored by the AMA, the American College of Obstetricians and Gynecologists, and other national professional groups.

Many physicians, however, use consultations of this kind as an opportunity to engage the girl in a candid discussion of her sexual behavior. It may alienate the patient for the physician to attempt a complete sexual inquiry when she comes for contraceptive advice, but a statement such as "This gives us a chance to discuss things you may not have been able to talk about before" may be followed by his asking whether she would not like to have such a dialogue with him, either during the current visit or at some future session.

In dealing with a patient who faces an unexpected and unwanted out-of-wedlock pregnancy, the physician will need to assess what pressures she is under—from her parents, the child's father, and others. He will explore her attitudes toward possible alternate courses of action in respect to the future of the child. If she is too disturbed to exercise objective judgment, he must work toward rapport, postponing the discussion of alternatives to a later time. He will be careful not to impose his own solutions just when she is most malleable and perhaps even eager to turn the decision-making over to someone else. The value of getting more information about the circumstances surrounding the pregnancy should be weighed, since disclosure of some of the particulars could cause the patient considerable pain without yielding very much that would be useful in dealing with the situation at hand. Most physicians will look for a chance to provide contraceptive advice for the future, and Chapter 6 adds relevant material on the subject.

Other fears about sex. The physician may find that the patient who fears sex fears it because it is perceived as an act of violence. A woman may perceive the penis as an instrument of mutilation, and be concerned about damage to her body during pregnancy or childbirth. A man may fear either giving or receiving physical injury during intercourse. The best clues to such misperceptions are afforded by the patient's fantasies during masturbation or coitus and the dreams that follow coitus. Any history of actual or feared incest or rape or any exposure in childhood to stories of mutilation may reveal the source of such fears. Occasionally an irrational fear of sex has been prompted by the first sight of menstrual blood.

Moral anxiety and the conviction that sexual activity is sinful, dirty or nasty can block sexual arousal, excitement and orgasm. On the other hand, an admission to oneself that the sex act is highly pleasurable can increase the burden of guilt to the point where one is frozen by inhibition or terrified of "deserved" punishment. The disclosure of such fears and attitudes during the interview will depend on the skill of the physician and his knowledge of the dynamic processes involved. Out of such knowledge he will frame his questions.

The fear of being homosexual is common, and occasionally is justified.

The patient who uses drugs

The interviewer should not overlook the possibility that the use of drugs may account for some of the sexual problems brought to him. Since drugs generally inhibit sexual performance more than they inhibit sexual arousal or excitement, it is well for the physician to ask about any drug intake in specific detail, and to be prepared for a variety of replies. He should also inquire about the use of alcohol and amphetamines. The effects of oral contraceptives on sexual responsiveness and performance are not clearly understood, but it seems evident that in some persons they decrease sexual drive and response. When psychic energizers are taken for depression it should be borne in mind by the physician that concomitantly poor sexual response is more often due to the underlying depression than to the drugs. The physician must also take into account that while marihuana seldom makes startling alterations in the sexual experience and has an uncertain pharmacologic influence, it may provide heightened awareness of bodily processes accompanied by some indifference to the relationship itself.

Homosexuality in the single person

If the patient interview elicits the fact that the patient is homosexual in his or her primary desire or action, it is important to explore the type and dimensions of sexual attitudes and activity just as with the heterosexual patient. The physician will want to determine whether or not the patient perceives his homosexuality as a problem, and whether or not it is a preferred mode of sexual activity. If it clearly is the preferred mode, what difficulties, if any, does the patient experience? Is he ashamed of himself, or is he able to identify himself openly and validly as a homosexual? If he is not willing to avow his homosexuality openly, is he able to disclose it to close friends and to his parents? Does he enjoy a reasonably gratifying social and sex life? Is the type of homosexual activity one that is likely to embroil him in legal or social difficulties? Does he find it necessary to frequent public places in the hope of attracting strangers, thus putting himself in the position of a degraded person who may provoke physical attack or prosecution by law?

If the patient wishes to amend his homosexuality, referral to a psychiatrist with special experience in this area is indicated. In that instance the physician may want to assess the general likelihood of successful treatment. He will want to know the extent of conflict aroused in the patient by his homosexual behavior, the degree of motivation for change, whether or not he has had any heterosexual experiences, and whether or not he has shown a capacity for self-discipline and has a good work history.

It was indicated in Chapter 1 that the interview of a homosexual may present particular difficulties for both doctor and patient. The physician will benefit by having read enough on the subject to be fully aware of its dimensions, and he will do well to avail himself of the learning opportunity afforded when representatives of the "Gay Liberation" offer to discuss their point of view and life styles.

Patients preferentially heterosexual but in doubt about their sexual identity give special concern. Adolescent fears of homosexuality may be awakened by sexual play with peers, which has in some measure involved at least one out of every three boys and many girls, as indicated briefly in Chapter 2. The interviewer should uncover the background of this sex play, the quality of peer pressure brought to bear, and the nature of the patient's fantasies during masturbation. Information about any heterosexual activity that may have taken place should also be sought. Often a timid or nonathletic boy who may have been called "sissy" or "queer" will reveal fears of being a homosexual in later life, but his anxiety is usually more closely involved with male rivalry than with sexual feelings. It may be possible for the physician to reassure his patient that what was perceived as homosexual activity was just one step in sexual development. This reassurance, when conveyed to a frightened adolescent, may give such relief that no further consultation is necessary, although psychotherapy may be indicated. In some cases it is certainly worth considering that the doubts expressed by the patient may have arisen from some failure in an area which is essentially nonsexual but to which the youngster has attached sexual significance.

The minority singles

In the general category of the single patient appear the spinster, the separated, divorced or widowed, and the aging bachelor—

all of whom labor under a minority status in contemporary society. Their expectations of themselves and others, and the light in which they are generally regarded, set them apart. Any physician who interviews these "singles" should avoid stereotyping them in the belief that every divorcee is sexually frustrated and "on the make," or that every middle-aged bachelor is too much attached to his mother, and latently homosexual. Conversely, it would be a mistake to assume an absence of sexual interest and activity in people who may or may not have had extensive sexual experience in the past, whatever their current status.

Premarital and couple counseling

However widely premarital counseling has been accepted, the opportunities it offers have been sadly neglected by physicians. Clergymen have been relatively more effective in this area, but few have been trained to be competent sex counselors, so that premarital counseling in general has done little up to the present to prevent the sexual problems that can arise before or during marriage. Yet the premarital examination and interview given by the physician provide an excellent opportunity for contraceptive counseling, for allaying anxieties about sex, and for minimizing sexual inhibition. If the physician is not in a position to provide this kind of counseling, he should be sure to make referral to an appropriate professional.

The physician's first task is to ascertain the attitudes of the couple toward sexuality and the quality of their sexual behavior toward one another. His object is (1) to provide suitable contraceptive advice and (2) to prevent future sexual dysfunction. Legal regulations requiring medical proof of freedom from venereal disease give the physician the chance of seeing each partner separately. This is a real advantage where the partners have not been candid with each other about their past sexual experiences or about what could prove to be more important considerations, their sexual attitudes and expectations. Concern of one partner about the past sexual history of the other is often intense, as is anxiety and doubt about what to reveal of one's own past in view of the unpredictability of the other's reaction to such disclosures. Although complete honesty can, and often does, lay a sound basis for an ongoing relationship entered into in good faith, it is always possible that a surprise disclosure will provoke serious resentment, guilt or feelings of inadequacy, so that the physician is generally safer in advising caution.

Conjoint interviewing of the couple will follow. Being careful not to betray confidences, the interviewer may work toward reconciling incompatible expectations. It is appropriate to discuss what each anticipates of the wedding night and the honeymoon, since the wedding night is all too often a disaster when either partner expects too much of himself or the other. If they learn in counseling that it could take a year or more of living together to achieve entirely gratifying sexual adjustment, this realization will minimize any dismay or disappointment experienced durng the honeymoon.

Sex is not the sole focus of premarital counseling, which should promote an exchange of views about other family issues —work, money, living arrangements, and so on. Some couples have never talked or even seriously thought about the number of children they want or how they want to space them. The physician may be the one to initiate the discussion. Throughout, the physician's primary role is to facilitate communication between the partners on matters of importance to them. The physician who does this skillfully will be laying the groundwork for his future role as a trusted adviser during the couple's married life.

The interviewer must keep his own views in abeyance until he has achieved a firm rapport with his patients, and he must accept them as they are at the time of the interview, however sharp the contrast revealed in the sexual interview between his own values and those of his patients. He may unconsciously envy his young, liberated patients, regretting that the sexual revolution came too late for him; or he may be deeply disturbed by youngsters who view sex as little more than recreation. Nevertheless, he will ask all questions from a neutral position and will resist any tendency to manifest personal discomfort in his interviewing. As mentioned elsewhere, skill comes with practice!

5

INTERVIEWING THE OLDER PERSON

Persistence of sexual interest

It is characteristic of our society to forget—or actually not to know—that sexual feelings and desires do not disappear in the elderly, but may for a number of reasons actually increase in intensity. The generation gap and the incredulity with which young people regard the possibility of this persistent sexuality in their elders constitute one of the problems involved in taking the sexual history of an older patient, especially one old enough to evoke the remembrance of a parental figure.

A number of recent studies indicate that any history of the elderly patient which fails to take his sexual life into account is incomplete. One study reports that while an overall pattern of decline in sexual interest and activity among old people was found in the sample, sex continued to play an important part in the lives of a considerable majority.

The physical or social status of a patient may justify postponing the taking of a sexual history—as, for example, when the patient's physical complaint is so severe that anything else is secondary, or when appropriate rapport has yet to be established. It should not be forgotten, however. The fact that the patient has a debilitating disease, has outlived his sexual partner, or is tied to a sick or incompetent sexual partner does not justify the physician's failure to obtain his sexual history.

Overprotection by the children. The way in which the elderly patient's children, who are often age peers of the physician, may patronize or overprotect their parent can deflect the younger doctor from full consideration of the patient's own feelings and desires, and complicate the history-taking:

> CASE EXAMPLE 8: A 64-year-old widow whose husband had been dead for 3 years visited her family physician because of her increasing irritability and her "depression" of 3 months' duration. She had great confidence in him but, being in good physical health, had hesitated to bother him about her emotional upset. She had been living with her 35-year-old divorced daughter, an exceedingly intelligent, attractive and successful career woman, for about a year and had been caring for her young grandchildren.
>
> In the first interview the patient launched into a discourse on her own capacities and her desire for independence, expressing considerable resentment of her daughter's behavior, particularly her active social life. She then disclosed that she felt taken for granted and even exploited by the daughter, but added quickly that she felt loved and useful with the grandchildren.
>
> The physician asked her how and in what way she missed her husband. She claimed to have become quite accustomed to his absence. In response to a direct question about their sexual relationship she replied that it had been enjoyable, adding spontaneously, "Sex is no longer for me."
>
> It soon became evident that she still had a considerable interest in sex, and as a matter of fact was thinking of "dating" a man she had recently met at a club for senior citizens. She was somewhat coy about saying that she felt it ridiculous for a woman her age to think so much about sex, but admitted having feelings of guilt about it. Within a short time she had relaxed markedly and finally acknowledged having strong feelings of jealousy for her daughter about which she felt very guilty indeed. She also speculated whether her dependence on her daughter was not the "real" problem.

This woman definitely believed that sexual feelings were supposed to disappear with age. As the interview ended, she admitted in a most embarrassed manner that she had masturbated occasionally and that she felt most uncomfortable about this. During the next interview a week later, she talked mostly about her general resentment at being old, unwanted, a widow, and dependent on her successful daughter, who, she felt, looked down on her.

The following week the physician saw the daughter alone first, and then her mother. The daughter could admit that she certainly might inadvertently have taken her mother for granted, and confessed that it had never occurred to her that her mother might be jealous or might want a more active sexual or social life of her own. Both mother and daughter were then able to discuss their feelings and misunderstandings openly with each other, with obvious sympathy and even some humor.

Sexual activity after illness. A 63-year-old widower expressed his discomfiture at having his sexuality overlooked during his recovery from a severe bout of diabetic acidosis and cardiac decompensation with a suspected myocardial infarct by saying, "I could understand their not bothering about my sex life when I was so sick but I became quite irritated and insulted when they didn't seem interested in my questions after I got well."

This case points out the need of many older people after an illness to know what limitations, if any, their condition places on sexual activity. At any age the patient who has been physically ill is likely to feel anxiety about resuming sexual activity, and the physician who matter-of-factly but sympathetically discusses this aspect of the illness fully does his patient a real service. (Some authorities evaluate the expenditure of energy during intercourse as equivalent to that required to climb two flights of stairs.) This is particularly true with the older patient, who not only is more likely to have undergone a life-threatening crisis like a coronary, or a life-altering first experience of severe incapacity, but may be highly reluctant to confide his continuing interest in sex to a younger man because of the prevailing view that it is unbecoming to the later years.

Points for the interviewer of older patients

The following points may help the physician vis-a-vis his elderly patient:

> 1—The elderly patient may bring up sexual concerns spontaneously, especially if he has a family physician in whom he can confide. The widow described above had great confidence in her family physician, and as it turned out had no trouble in talking about very personal matters with him once she was able to push herself into making an appointment.

> 2—Elderly patients, despite their apparent experience, may be uninformed on many sexual issues. They are more reluctant than the young to admit their ignorance and to ask questions, so that the initiative falls on the physician.

> 3—The elderly patient is generally more pleased and flattered than resentful at questions about his sexual life. The symbolic aspects of sex, as well as the actual realities of sexual behavior, have social meaning, and it can seem demeaning to the patient to be considered as lacking in sexual identity. This is one of the reasons for obtaining a sexual history even when the patient's condition obviously renders him incapable of sexual activity.

> 4—Elderly people are often irritable and angry as they endure their loss or reduction of function, their illnesses, their dependency, loneliness, and the condescending or rejecting treatment of family members. They often strongly resent the conditions of their life but feel guilty about their resentment. This guilt is often so intense and so painful that it accounts for much of the depression so common among the aged. Sexual feelings or im-

pulses that persist into old age, when considered no longer permissible, can significantly intensify this guilt, and be the straw that breaks the camel's back. It often has a remarkably dramatic and beneficial effect on the well-being of the patient to relieve his guilt over sexual matters. It is well to remember that the elderly are deprived of many gratifications and frequently are not sufficiently adaptable or flexible to find substitute gratifications without help.

5—Aging, at least in Western society, often involves a loss of self-esteem. The older patient's adoption of a superior, parental attitude toward the young is a natural defense against this loss, but it is highly unacceptable to the young physician or medical student, who may be sensitive to reminders that he is young and inexperienced. The physician who can recognize his patient's arrogance as a defense against this loss and deal with it can usually conduct a pleasant and productive interview where he would meet defeat in the absence of such recognition.

6—As indicated, there is almost no chance of hurting or insulting the elderly patient by an effort to take a sexual history. The patient should be assured, even when there are many medical problems, that sex is still a permissible and appropriate interest for him, and the examiner should be able to determine whether any psychological distress the patient displays is based on sexual problems.

The examiner may, on the other hand, find that many of the problems he supposed to be sexual in his elderly patients are not primarily sexual but expressions of more painful feelings—anxiety, loneliness, frustration, anger and guilt, compounded by the loss in old age of former resources and gratifications. With the sexual component forthrightly acknowledged, the physician may work with his patient on the fundamental problem of adapting to old age in as realistically effective a way as possible while maximizing possibilities for pleasure and independence.

6

SPECIAL CONSIDERATIONS FOR THE INTERVIEWER

Masked sexual problems

The physician or surgeon adequately trained in taking a sexual history can often identify by brief questioning the presence of sexual problems underlying many physical complaints, although the patient may be unaware of these reasons for his complaint, or may be too much embarrassed to volunteer what insight he has. Complaints of hot flashes, headache, loss of appetite, abdominal pain, insomnia, or generalized emotional distress are typical examples.

Even in this enlightened age many people are ashamed to acknowledge sexual problems when they suspect that sexual frustration may account for their emotional malaise. An example might be the menopausal woman who has given up intercourse at a time when she is particularly free for its enjoyment, out of consideration for her husband's hypertensive condition, which she believes contraindicates sexual activity.

Generalized panic. A psychiatrist is needed only in the most difficult diagnostic and treatment situations. Referral of routine sexual problems such as those described in the following generally reflects the physician's unwillingness to take the responsibility, or his inability to do so, based on the inadequacy of his medical education in sexuality.

CASE EXAMPLE 9: A 14-year-old boy was brought to the emergency ward of a city hospital by his father because the boy panicked and expressed the fear that "something terrible" was about to happen to him. He was unable to tell anyone, even his sympathetic father, what he feared. The intern who examined and questioned him first could find nothing wrong with him except the anxiety, and called the resident, who suggested taking a more detailed history.

This disclosed the fact that the patient was sexually attracted by a young girl and that an erection experienced while kissing her had alarmed him with fears of damage to his penis. He had been brought up strictly in matters of sex, and with religious teachings that masturbation could harm his penis. He had been masturbating guiltily for several years, and his sexual interest in the girl had reawakened the old threats and fears in sufficient strength to account for his present panic.

A brief psychotherapeutic intervention of three or four visits, focused chiefly on correcting misinformation about sexual matters, was enough to accomplish effective treatment of his problems.

Abdominal distress. A more specific somatic complaint was reported by a young married, childless woman in acute distress with lower abdominal pain and nausea.

CASE EXAMPLE 10: A 21-year-old married childless woman reported to the hospital emergency room in acute abdominal distress with nausea. The gynecologist found nothing physically wrong, but noted that she was tearful and apparently in considerable emotional distress. When he asked if anything had been troubling her, he discovered that a friend of hers had recently told her she was pregnant.

Further questioning revealed that the patient had been in love with her friend's husband, and imagined herself in the wife's place. She wished she were carrying this man's child and jealously wanted to destroy his wife or to deprive her of her pregnancy. Her acute abdominal symptoms came from her intense pregnancy wishes, jealous rage, and guilt.

Depression and insomnia. Sometimes a patient is only too ready to disclose a sexual problem if the physician is willing to ask questions and to listen.

> CASE EXAMPLE 11: A 20-year-old college sophomore complained to his physician of depression, loss of energy, and difficulty in sleeping. His outpatient medical work-up revealed no physical abnormality, but when his urinalysis showed a slight albuminuria he was admitted to the hospital for further study. The albuminuria proved to have no significance, but inquiry about his sexual history revealed a basic problem, as the following portion of the interview will show:

Doctor: Did you go out with girls in high scnool?
Patient: Yes. I was very popular with girls, but I didn't have much sexual experience.
Doctor: Have you been going out with anyone lately?
Patient: Yes. I've been dating a college girl for a while, but I can't satisfy her. She keeps trying to get me to satisfy her. . . . Her father and her older brother —they're both big business tycoons. I don't feel like much compared to them.
Doctor: What happens when you are with the girl?
Patient: Well, I have intercourse with her, but then I come too soon. I guess I'm anxious.
Doctor: And what happens then?
Patient: Well, she complains about not having an orgasm, and then I try harder, and the same thing happens. I try harder and harder until I get a pain in the balls. Sometimes I get so worried about failing again that I lose my erection.
Doctor: Then how do you feel?
Patient: Worse and worse.

At this point, the physician took a detailed sexual history that established the basis for the patient's conflicts about potency and sexual adequacy, which constituted his chief problem.

Insomnia of 2 years' duration. The identification of a sexual cause for an illness is not always made so readily. It must often await a more detailed sexual history.

> CASE EXAMPLE 12: A 30-year-old married woman consulted a physician for "difficulty in sleeping" of 2 years' duration. The physician in turn referred her to an able second-year psychiatric resident who obtained a great deal of useful information about the patient's childhood and family relationships, but she remained irritable and angry after 3 months and complained of feeling inadequate as a woman. She said she was fond of her husband but did not love him, adding that he was "not fertile." The resident brought the case to a different supervisor for a fresh look and the supervisor advised him to obtain a sexual history.
>
> In the sexual history the patient attributed her sleeping problem to sexual frustration, and admitted that "difficulty in sleeping" was a euphemism for her inability to have an orgasm. This problem was partly caused by inadequate penetration and activity on the part of her husband, who had Klinefelter's syndrome. She had known of his condition before their marriage and had agreed to marry him "out of pity." Manual manipulation of her external genitalia excited her but added to her frustration.

No approach to the serious neurosis that had led this women knowingly to choose such a mate was possible until the basic facts of her sexual history were obtained. Interestingly, the resident on the case complained of the inadequacy of his training in this area. Neither in medical school nor in the first year of his psychiatric residency had he received specific training in obtaining a sexual history.

Alcoholic binge of 9 days. Struggles over sexual feelings proved to be an important factor in the case of a man who falls into the category of those to whom the young physician does not attribute active sexuality.

CASE EXAMPLE 13: A 62-year-old man was admitted to the hospital in an acutely tremulous state with auditory hallucinations, after a 9-day alcoholic binge during the last 4 days of which he had eaten almost nothing. His hallucinations subsided promptly, but when he seemed to the medical resident to be depressed, a psychiatric consultation was scheduled and the following information obtained.

The patient had been reared in Ireland by Roman Catholic parents strict about sexual matters. At the age of 39 he came to this country and married a woman he had known and loved during his youth in Ireland but from whom he had been separated for many years. He drank a great deal of beer, and quarrels spoiled the marital relationship. The wife became mentally ill, and when he was 49 she was hospitalized with a schizophrenic illness which kept her continuously in the hospital.

As the years went by, she became increasingly withdrawn until she reached a point, shortly before the patient's admission, where she neither spoke to him nor seemed to recognize him. Although he was quite lonely, the patient regarded his marriage vows as sacred and turned to no other woman for love or companionship. He continued to drink steadily, but liquor was not a serious problem for him.

Several months before his admission to the hospital the patient rented a room in his house to a young woman separated from her husband. He found himself attracted to her and felt guilt over his sexual feelings. He became more troubled when she had parties in her apartment which he thought of as "sexual orgies." One day while intoxicated she embraced him and kissed him on the mouth. He felt a rush of excitement but was unable to obtain an erection because of his guilt and anxiety. He thought to himself, "I'm finished." His drunken binge, about which he was later greatly ashamed, followed this incident. A combination of stresses—loneliness, sadness over losing his wife, guilt over his unacceptable sexual feelings and, finally, an "impotence" he could not understand—precipitated his alcoholic spree.

In this case the patient did not voluntarily speak of his sexual preoccupations. It took detailed questioning to uncover the fact that his acute episode was related to disturbing sexual thoughts and feelings.

Problems surrounding reproduction

Contraception. The specific issues involved in providing contraception for the unmarried girl have been discussed in an earlier chapter. Equally important issues must be considered in providing contraceptive advice to those who are married and perhaps already parents. It should not be left to the obstetrician-gynecologist to offer sound information about the various methods and agents of contraception and their use and effectiveness. It is not unusual for a patient who is unhappy about being pregnant to reveal in response to skillful questioning her ignorance about contraceptive measures or about some aspect crucial to their effective use.

The physician will want to inform himself about what contraceptive measures his patient has been in the habit of using. It is possible that a certain contraceptive reduces the couple's sexual gratification, or that they are in some other way involved in a sexual problem. A physician asked about a proposed change in contraceptive method should be able to explain the advantages and disadvantages of the various methods and to comment on the effectiveness of each. He will be interested in the reason underlying the proposal for change— whether they hope for improvement in sexual gratification or for more trustworthy prevention of pregnancy. And his questioning should certainly not overlook the possibility that a psychological struggle is taking place, a struggle in which one partner is trying to get the other to assume the responsibility for contraception or to bear the burden of it.

Pregnancy. A full exploration of the situation and attitudes of the pregnant woman, whether single or married, deserves more detailed discussion than that given in Chapter 4.

When seeing his pregnant patient, the physician will want to ascertain how she found out she was pregnant, how far advanced the pregnancy is, her husband's attitude toward it as well as her own, and whether it was planned or unplanned. Exaggerated symptoms may be the clue to an underlying sexual problem, even when they represent the reactions more or less to be expected, like first-trimester nausea or third-trimester "heaviness." When the husband feels awkward with his pregnant wife and tends to shy away from her, she may be greatly distressed. As she herself turns more and more inward during her pregnancy, it may be the husband who feels rejected and he who becomes angry or retaliative. If he turns away from his wife it may be because he finds her less appealing sexually, or because he believes it wrong, inappropriate or unwise for her to have sexual intercourse at such a time. He may be consoling himself with another woman, or his wife may fear this possibility. And she may not express such concerns unless given the opportunity to do so and asked appropriate questions.

It is unfortunate that in many busy obstetrical clinics interviews are conducted in open booths that deny the patient the privacy she should have in revealing matters important both to her and to her physician. Many of the concerns and problems of the pregnant woman are personal and intimate, often laden with sexual connotations. The need to provide privacy for these interviews cannot be overstressed. It is also important for the physician to indicate that he has plenty of time for any disclosures the patient feels she wants to make.

The physician should be prepared to answer a variety of common questions on the basis of knowledge rather than answering them on the basis of prejudice, hearsay or folklore. When he is asked a question to which he has no firm and well-informed reply, he should confess the limitations of his knowledge and follow through by obtaining an answer from an informed obstetrician. Among such questions might be questions about breast-feeding or the advisability of intercourse during different stages of the pregnancy and in the postpartum period. It is important to know how the woman feels about breast-feeding, and to prepare her for its erotic possibilities, since these provide pleasure for the accepting woman but distress the one taken by surprise with a reaction which she regards as wrong or distasteful on moral grounds.

Abortion. When a woman wants an abortion, or asks for help in deciding whether or not to have one, the physician will be wise to approach the matter objectively, obtaining all possible information that will help him discuss the issues profitably with his patient. The ground covered in his inquiry, the order of his questions and their phrasing will depend on how much anxiety the patient displays, the degree of rapport he establishes with her, her own style, and the amount of support required of him in the interview. The physician must find out why the patient seeks an abortion and whether her reasons give medical indications or contraindications for this procedure. As indicated earlier, he should know whether the abortion is the patient's idea or whether it is being advocated by someone else. If she is married, is it her husband's wish to terminate the pregnancy? If so, is his preference dictated by an income level inadequate to support another child, fear that the child will come between him and his wife, or a feeling that the marriage is too unstable to risk bringing a child—or another child—into the picture?

An insight into the woman's sexual maturity, her personality strengths and vulnerabilities, her mental and emotional stability, will help the physician assess the medical or psychiatric indications for the abortion, and any likelihood that psychological problems connected with the abortion will arise after it has been performed. He will, of course, have familiarized himself with any renal or cardiac problem the patient may have, and with any other possible physical contraindications to completion of the pregnancy.

Sterilization. Consulted about sterilization for either a woman or a man, the physician must find out why it is being contemplated and what efforts have been made to solve the problem by contraception. Whenever a man is seriously considering sterilization, the doctor should assess the insights of both husband and wife into the emotional implications of this procedure and their appreciation of the probability that it will be irreversible. The physical and emotional implications of a sterilization of the woman should also be explored with both the patient and her husband before endorsing this course. The final decision should most certainly involve both partners.

Sexual problems more apparent than real

One reason why the physician should have a wide knowledge of sexuality—including possible nonsexual uses of sex—when he takes a sexual history is that the patient may err in ascribing a sexual origin to his problem. This is sometimes the case when the patient is ignorant or confused about some of the specifics of sex, or does not understand the range of human sexual functioning. The four examples which follow illustrate situations in which the core problem is *not* sexual:

Pseudohomosexuality. History-taking itself in this situation can be therapeutic. As indicated in Chapter 4 many adolescents, and some adults as well, are deeply concerned at the possibility that they are homosexual. Such anxiety may arise from a normal, human feeling of affection for friends of the same sex; a basic lack of security in one's own identity; or increasing external pressures that feed the need to be cared for by someone else. Proper consideration should be given to this anxiety by the physician who interviews the patient. When true homosexuality is not the issue, the physician will shift the focus away from the purported sexual problem and toward some of the related nonsexual issues that need clarification.

Sexual symptoms heralding mental disorder. Undue concern about sexuality can herald the onset of mental disorder. A young man presenting with the complaint that he is turning into a homosexual may be experiencing the first phase of a psychotic decompensation. As the history is taken, the patient's line of thinking in this and other matters will usually disclose thought disorder or other symptoms of a schizophrenic illness. Impotence or loss of interest in sexuality may indicate depression. An alertness to this possibility will lead the physician to an awareness of other indications of the depressive state such as sleeplessness, early-morning awakening, anorexia, rumination, or preoccupation with suicide.

Inaccurately described premature ejaculation. The patient complaining of inadequate sexual performance may be ignorant about sex, or he may lack information about some specifics of sexual behavior. Occasionally a man will complain of premature ejaculation when in actuality he is able to sustain intravaginal intercourse for many minutes, having penetrated his partner without enough foreplay to provide her with a climax. So much has been written in the popular press about the importance of simultaneous orgasm in intercourse that many men feel that they are inadequate as men and lovers unless they can evoke orgasm in their partner. Their women may confirm these views. It is also possible that the female partner suffers from "frigidity." Such situations, though not necessarily based on fact, emphasize the involvement of both partners in the responsibility for successful sexual union.

Pseudo-inadequacy in the woman. Another complaint made on the basis of misinformation is that of a woman deploring her inability to have multiple orgasm. Having heard that all very sexual women experience them, she feels that she is not "normal" when she does not. The physician will weigh the susceptibility of the situation to the simple solution of explaining that people differ in their sexual response and that the range of sexual performance is very wide. The possibility that the woman suffers dissatisfaction in the single orgasm, or, indeed, never feels satisfied, should of course be considered. In some cases it will become clear that her partner expects her to have multiple orgasm as evidence of his effective masculinity, and that he has displaced his feelings of inadequacy onto her. Confirming again the fact that it takes two capable partners to achieve a successful sexual union, an exploration of the underlying situation may identify the partner who is not consulting the physician as the one who really needs help.

7

SUMMARY

Although the skill to assess sexual function in his patient and the importance it occupies in his patient's life is a highly useful one for the physician, medical schools have all too often failed to help him acquire it. Fortunately, this scholastic shortcoming is rapidly being corrected.

As in any other area of medicine, the successful evaluation made possible by skillful interviewing depends on a knowledge of the structure and function of that aspect of life being investigated. A sexual history is obtained in basically the same way as any other medical history. However, discussion of sexual matters is apt to be hampered by the attitudes of both physician and patient because of the emotional investment of the parties and the complexity of sociocultural considerations involved. An informed understanding of sexuality and a resolution of his own anxieties and inhibitions concerning sexuality will permit the physician to become relaxed and to conduct an effective interview, and this in turn will facilitate patient response. Even when the physician is reasonably comfortable with and generally knowledgeable about sexual matters, it is important that he be aware of the extent to which open communication can be blocked by cross-cultural, ethnic, and social differences, as well as a difference in age.

However, the physician who becomes knowledgeable about the subject and strives to improve communication with his patients will ultimately find to his satisfaction that his ability to reduce suffering and to promote normal function has been considerably enhanced. A successful interview about sexual problems can be in itself therapeutic, since it permits ventilation of difficulties the patient has heretofore been unable to assess, to share, or perhaps even to put into words. As mentioned, the interviewing situation may vary greatly from patient to patient, depending on the patient's age, his circumstances, and whether or not he is aware of his sexual problems. Often the physician's careful and knowledgeable exploration of the patient's sexual life will clarify otherwise mysterious medical complaints. The physician interested in his patient's general well-being will discover that any understanding of impediments to it is difficult without an awareness of the patient's sexual state, so integral to the whole organism.

Besides being occupied in the traditional way with the treatment of disease, the medical profession becomes daily more concerned with health as a positive state. The physician will be increasingly interested in adding a sexual evaluation to the other assessments of his patient's condition, and will become better able to provide guidance that will lay the groundwork for a more complete and healthy life for his patient.

Despite the fact that clergymen, psychologists, social workers and marriage counselors are frequently consulted about sexual problems, the physician remains the person most commonly regarded as an authority on the subject. Thus his responsibility for helping to alleviate suffering by improving sexual functioning seems inescapable.

APPENDIX A:

TOPICS COVERED IN A SEXUAL HISTORY *

The outline which follows indicates the lines of inquiry to be considered in obtaining a sexual history. It is not intended as a questionnaire to which patients should be subjected. Depending on the individual clinical situation, one or more lines of inquiry in this comprehensive review of possible topics could be sufficient and appropriate.

I—IDENTIFYING DATA

A—*Patient*
1) age
2) sex
3) marital status (single, number of times previously married, currently married, separated, divorced, remarried)

B—*Parents*
1) ages
2) dates of death and ages at death
3) birthplace
4) marital status (married, separated, divorced or remarried)
5) religion
6) education
7) occupation
8) congeniality
9) demonstration of affection
10) feelings toward parents

C—*Siblings* (as indicated)

D—*Marital partner*
1) age
2) marital status (number of times previously married; remarried, if divorced)
3) place of birth
4) religion
5) education
6) occupation
7) cultural background

---

* This outline is based on the Sexual Performance Evaluation Questionnaire of the Marriage Council of Philadelphia. The Council is affiliated with the Division of Family Study, Department of Psychiatry, University of Pennsylvania School of Medicine, 4025 Chestnut Street, Philadelphia, Pennsylvania 19104.

E—*Children*
1) ages
2) sex
3) assets
4) problems

II—CHILDHOOD SEXUALITY

A—*Family attitudes about sex*
1) degree of parents' openness or reserve about sex
2) parents' attitudes about nudity and modesty
3) behavior about nudity and modesty: (a) parents; (b) patient

B—*Learning about sex*
1) Asking parents about sex: (a) which parent; (b) answers given; (c) at what age; (d) nature of questions; (e) feelings about it
2) Information volunteered by parents: (a) which parent; (b) what information; (c) at what age; (d) feelings about it
3) Explanations by either parent (indicate which parent or parent substitute): (a) sex play; (b) pregnancy; (c) birth; (d) intercourse; (e) masturbation; (f) nocturnal emissions; (g) menstruation; (h) homosexuality; (i) venereal disease; (j) age at time of each explanation; (k) feelings about such learning

C—*Childhood sex activity*
1) First sight of nude body of same sex: (a) age ("how young"); (b) feelings; (c) circumstances
2) Of opposite sex: (a) age ("how young"); (b) feelings; (c) circumstances
3) Genital self-stimulation: (a) age ("how young") *before adolescence* at 1st occurrence; (b) manner; (c) orgasm? (how often?); (d) feelings (pleasure, guilt); (e) consequences, if apprehended
4) Other solitary sexual activities (bathroom sensual activity regarding urine, feces, odors)
5) First sexual exploration or play (playing doctor) with another child (possible reply may be *never*): (a) age; (b) sex and age of other child; (c) nature of activity (looking, manual touching, genital touching, vaginal penetration, oral-genital contact, anal contact, other; (d) feelings (pleasure, guilt); (e) consequences, if apprehended (what and by whom)
6) Other episodes of sexual exploration or play with other children *before adolescence* (subcategories as in #5 above)
7) Sex activity with older persons: (a) at what ages; (b) ages of

other persons; (c) nature of activity; (d) willing or unwilling;
(e) force or actual attack involved? (f) feelings

D—*Primal scene*
1) Parents' intercourse: (a) hearing; (b) seeing; (c) feelings
2) Other than parents: (a) hearing; (b) seeing; (c) feelings

E—*Childhood sexual theories or myths*
1) Thoughts about conception and birth
2) Functions of male and female genitals in sexuality
3) Roles of other body orifices or parts (e.g., umbilicus) in sexuality and reproduction (e.g., oral impregnation, anal intercourse, anal birth, pregnancy by kissing, etc.)

F—*Other childhood sexuality*

III—ONSET OF ADOLESCENCE

A—*In girls*
1) Preparation for menstruation: (a) informant; (b) nature of information; (c) age given; (d) feelings about way in which the information was given; (e) about the information itself
2) Age: (a) at first period; (b) when breasts began developing; (c) of appearance of pubic and axillary hair
3) Menstruation: (a) regularity (initial, subsequent, present); (b) frequency; (c) discomfort? (d) medication? (e) duration; (f) hygienic method (Kotex, tampons); (g) feelings about first period (surprise, distaste, interest, anticipation, guilt, shyness); (h) about subsequent periods

B—*In boys*
1) Preparation for adolescence: (a) informant; (b) nature of information; (c) age given
2) Age: (a) of appearance of pubic and axillary hair; (b) change of voice; (c) of first orgasm; (d) with or without ejaculation; (e) frequency of orgasm; (f) for how many years?
3) Emotional reaction: (a) to early or delayed onset of adolescence; (b) to first orgasm

IV—ORGASTIC EXPERIENCES

A—*Nocturnal emissions (male) or orgasm during sleep (female)*
1) Frequency: (a) premarital; (b) postmarital
2) Accompanying dreams

B—*Masturbation*
1) Age when begun
2) Ever punished?
3) Frequency per week: (a) during teens; (b) during twenties; (c) during thirties, etc.
4) Method: (a) usual; (b) others tried; (c) others used
5) Marital partner's knowledge of past or present masturbation
6) Practiced with others: (a) before marriage; (b) with spouse
7) Emotional reactions
8) Accompanying fantasies

C—*Necking and petting ("making out")*
1) Age when begun
2) Frequency
3) Number of partners
4) Types of activity

D—*Intercourse* (see also section IX below)
1) Frequency of occurrence
2) Number of partners
3) Kinds of partners (fiancee, lover, friend, prostitute, unselective)
4) Contraceptives used
5) Feelings about premarital intercourse: (a) for girls; (b) for boys; (c) for different ages

E—*Orgastic frequency (overall)*
1) During teens
2) During twenties
3) During thirties
4) During forties, etc.

V—FEELINGS ABOUT SELF AS MASCULINE/FEMININE

A—*The male patient*
1) Does he feel masculine?
2) Popular?
3) Sexually adequate?
4) Any feelings about being a "sissy?"
5) Does he feel accepted by his peers? (belongs to a group?)
6) Feelings about: (a) body size (height, weight, etc.); (b) appearance (handsomeness, virility); (c) voice; (d) hair distribution; (e) genitalia (size, circumcision, undescended testicle, virility, potency, ability to respond sexually); (f) cross-dressing (any experience in doing so)

B—*The female patient*
1) Does she feel feminine?
2) Popular?
3) Sexually adequate?
4) Was she ever a "tomboy"?
5) Does she feel accepted by her peers? (belongs to a group)
6) Feelings about: (a) body size (height, weight, etc.); (b) appearance (beauty); (c) breast size, hips; (d) distribution of hair; (e) cross-dressing (any experience in doing so)

VI—SEXUAL FANTASIES AND DREAMS

A—*Nature of sex dreams*

B—*Nature of fantasies*
1) During masturbation
2) During intercourse

VII—DATING

A—*Age* ("how young")
1) First date
2) First kissing: (a) lips; (b) deep
3) First petting or "making out": feelings
4) First "going steady": feelings

B—*Frequency:* feelings about frequency of dating

VIII—ENGAGEMENT

A—*Age* (formal or informal?)

B—*Sex activity during engagement period*
1) With fiancee: (a) kissing; (b) petting; (c) intercourse
2) With others: (a) number of individuals; (b) frequency; (c) nature of activity

IX—MARRIAGE

A—*Vital statistics*
1) Date of marriage
2) Age: (a) interviewee; (b) spouse
3) Spouse's occupation
4) Is spouse present at interview?
5) Previous marriage(s): (a) interviewee; (b) spouse

    6) Reason for termination of previous marriage (death, divorce):
       (a) interviewee; (b) spouse
    7) Number, sex and ages of children from previous marriage:
       (a) interviewee; (b) spouse

B—*Premarital sex with spouse* (if not previously covered)
    1) Petting: (a) frequency; (b) feelings about it
    2) Intercourse: (a) frequency; (b) feelings about it
    3) Contraceptives (identify kind used, if any)

C—*Wedding trip (honeymoon)*
    1) Social and geographic particulars: (a) where; (b) duration;
       (c) generally pleasant or unpleasant?
    2) Sexual considerations: (a) frequency of intercourse; (b) was
       sex pleasant or unpleasant? (c) was the wife aroused? (d)
       was orgasm achieved (occasionally, always, never)? (e) was
       spouse considerate? (f) any complications (impotence, frigid-
       ity, pain, difficulty in penetration, "honeymoon" cystitis)

D—*Sex in marriage*
    1) General satisfaction or dissatisfaction
    2) Thoughts about general satisfaction or dissatisfaction of
       spouse

E *Pregnancies*
    1) Number
    2) At what ages
    3) Results (normal births, Caesarian delivery, miscarriages, abor-
       tions)
    4) Effects on sexual adjustment (fear of pregnancy)
    5) Number wanted and number unwanted
    6) Sex of child wanted or unwanted

X—EXTRAMARITAL SEX

A—*Emotional attachments*
    1) Number of different attachments
    2) Frequency of contacts
    3) Feelings about extramarital emotional attachment

B—*Sexual intercourse*
    1) Number of different partners
    2) Frequency of incidents
    3) Feelings about extramarital intercourse

C—*Postmarital masturbation*
  1) Frequency
  2) How recent?

D—*Postmarital homosexuality*
  1) Frequency
  2) How recent?

E—*Multiple sex ("swinging")*

XI—SEX AFTER WIDOWHOOD, SEPARATION OR DIVORCE

A—*Outlet*
  1) Orgasms in sleep
  2) Masturbation
  3) Petting
  4) Intercourse
  5) Homosexuality
  6) Other

B—*Frequency of past or current resort to outlet*

C—*Feelings about such experiences*

XII—SEXUAL DEVIATIONS

A—*Homosexuality*
  1) First experience: (a) age ("how young"); (b) age and number of persons involved; (c) how often repeated; (d) nature of activity (looking, manual, oral, anal); (e) active or passive (in seeking the activity, in performance)? (f) circumstances (childhood sex play, seduction by elders)
  2) During and since adolescence: (a) patient's age; (b) age and number of persons involved; (c) frequency; (d) recency; (e) nature of activity (looking, manual, oral, anal); (f) usual circumstances (at movies or gay bars, in public toilets or turkish baths, with minors); (g) penalties (blackmail, being "rolled," being arrested); (h) interest or desire and whether fulfilled or unfulfilled

B—*Sexual contact with animals*
  1) When: (a) childhood; (b) in adolescence; (c) since adolescence
  2) Nature of contact: (a) vaginal penetration; (b) anal penetration; (c) licking by animal; (d) masturbation on or of an animal

3) Frequency
4) Recency
5) Feelings about sexual contact with animals

C—*Voyeurism*

1) Interest or pleasure in looking at objects connoting sex (genitals, nudes, etc.): (a) in childhood; (b) in adolescence; (c) since adolescence; (d) frequency; (e) recency; (f) circumstances; (g) consequences; (h) arousal or masturbation while looking

2) Sexual interest or pleasure from looking into mirror: (a) in childhood; (b) in adolescence; (c) since adolescence; (d) frequency; (e) recency

3) Interest in pornographic pictures: (a) in childhood; (b) during adolescence; (c) since adolescence; (d) frequency; (e) recency; (f) feelings about them (pleasure, disgust); (g) response (arousal, masturbation)

4) Peeping: (a) in childhood; (b) in adolescence; (c) since adolescence; (d) frequency; (e) recency; (f) circumstances (in bathhouses, public toilets, lighted windows at night, by use of field glasses, etc.); (g) consequences, if apprehended; (h) feelings about peeping

D—*Exhibitionism* (deriving pleasure from displaying genitals)

1) To whom: (a) children; (b) adults

2) When: (a) in childhood; (b) in adolescence; (c) since adolescence; (d) frequency; (e) recency; (f) circumstances (in bathhouses, public toilets, lighted windows at night, etc.); (g) consequences, if apprehended; (h) feelings about exhibitionism

E—*Fetishes, Tra svestism*

1) Nature of fetish (underwear, other clothing, or objects of sexual attraction): (a) when adopted; (b) sexual behavior associated with it (e.g., masturbation); (c) frequency; (d) recency; (e) consequences

2) Nature of transvestite activity: (a) when adopted; (b) sexual behavior associated with it; (c) frequency; (d) recency; (e) consequences

F—*Sadomasochism*

1) Nature of activity: (a) pain inflicted; (b) pain undergone; (c) means employed

2) Sexual response: (a) to activity itself; (b) to fantasies or such activity

3) Frequency

4) Recency

5) Consequences

G—*Seduction and Rape*

1) Has the patient seduced or raped another individual? (a) frequency; (b) recency; (c) circumstances; (d) consequences

2) Has the patient been seduced or raped? (a) frequency; (b) recency; (c) circumstances; (d) consequences

H—*Incest*

1) Nature of sex play or sexual activity with: (a) brother; (b) sister; (c) mother; (d) father; (e) son; (f) daughter; (g) other

2) Period of activity: (a) in childhood; (b) in adolescence; (c) since adolescence

3) Frequency

4) Recency

5) Consequences

J—*Prostitution*

1) Has patient accepted or paid money for sex: (a) when in life? (b) frequency; (c) recency

2) Has patient "rolled" someone or ever been "rolled"?

3) Feelings about prostitution

4) Types of sexual practices: (a) actual; (b) tolerated; (c) preferred

5) Types of clients accepted or paid for

XIII—CERTAIN EFFECTS OF SEX ACTIVITIES

A—*Venereal disease*

1) Age ("how young") of learning about venereal disease

2) Venereal disease contracted: (a) gonorrhea (when, treatment, effects); (b) syphilis (when, treatment, effects)

B—*Illegitimate pregnancy*

1) Having an illegitimate pregnancy (female patient): (a) how often; (b) at what age; (c) disposition of pregnancy (miscarriage, abortion, adoption, marriage; kept baby; kept baby without marriage); (d) feelings about it

2) Causing an illegitimate pregnancy (male patient); (a) how often; (b) at what age; (c) disposition of pregnancy; (d) feelings about it

C—*Abortion*
1) Why performed?
2) At what age(s)?
3) How often?
4) Before or after marriage?
5) Circumstances: (a) who; (b) where; (c) how
6) Feelings about abortion: (a) at the time; (b) in retrospect; (c) "anniversary reaction"

XIV—USE OF EROTIC MATERIAL

A—*Response to erotic or pornographic literature, pictures, movies·*
1) Sexual pleasure arousal
2) Mild pleasure
3) Disinterest
4) Disgust

B—*Use in connection with sexual activity*
1) Type of material
2) Frequency of use
3) Use accompanying or preceding: (a) intercourse; (b) masturbation; (c) other sexual activity

APPENDIX B:

SEXUAL PERFORMANCE EVALUATION *

This evaluation outline is intended, like the sexual history outline (Appendix A), as an indication of possible lines of inquiry. It is not intended to be used exhaustively or in rote fashion. Note that although this outline was designed for married couples, it is appropriate for any couple.

Case No. _____   Interviewer _____

Date schedule filled out _____

Schedule filled out before ( ), during ( ) or after ( ) counseling on sexual adjustment.

1. Are you satisfied with the sexual adjustment in your marriage? Do you think your spouse is satisfied?

	Yourself	Spouse
a—Yes	( )	( )
b—No	( )	( )
c—Mixed feelings	( )	( )
d—Do not know	( )	( )

Yourself: If not, what is not satisfactory to you? (See question 2 below.)
Spouse: If not, what do you think is not satisfactory to your spouse? (See question 2 following.)

2. Have you had any difficulty with any of the following?
   a—Techniques of petting and foreplay ( )
   b—Positions ( )
   c—Wife's inactivity ( )
   d—Wife does not achieve orgasm ( )
   e—Husband has difficulty with erection ( )
   f—Husband has orgasm too quickly ( )
   g—Painful intercourse ( )
   h—Fear of pregnancy ( )
   i—Husband wishes more frequent sexual activity than wife ( )
   j—Wife wishes more frequent sexual activity than husband ( )

* To be filled out by the patient. This evaluation form represents a modification of one used by the Marriage Council of Philadelphia, Inc., affiliated with the Division of Family Study, Department of Psychiatry, University of Pennsylvania School of Medicine, 4025 Chestnut Street, Philadelphia, Pennsylvania 19104.

k—Differences in attitudes toward sex   ( )
m—Fatigue   ( )
n—Lack of privacy   ( )
o—Interference with sex due to working hours   ( )
p—Other reasons (specify)   ( )
q—No difficulties   ( )

3. Have you been in touch with anyone for assistance with the sexual side of your marriage?
   a—No   ( )
   b—Yes   ( )
   c—If yes, how long ago? (1) Years   ( ) or (2) Months   ( )
   d—Check off the type of person or agency and whether you were helped:

	No help	Some help	A lot of help
1—Relative	( )	( )	( )
2—Friend	( )	( )	( )
3—Doctor	( )	( )	( )
4—Psychiatrist	( )	( )	( )
5—Social agency	( )	( )	( )
6—Clinical psychologist	( )	( )	( )
7—Clergyman (minister, priest, rabbi)	( )	( )	( )
8—Teacher	( )	( )	( )
9—Other (specify)	( )	( )	( )

4. How frequently, on the average, do you and your spouse have intercourse at present? (*Average* means typical or usual)
   a—No intercourse   ( )   f—3 times a week   ( )
   b—Less than once a month   g—4 times a week   ( )
      (specify)   ( )   h—5 times a week   ( )
   c—Once or twice a month   ( )   i—6 times a week   ( )
   d—Once a week   ( )   j—7 times a week or more   ( )
   e—Twice a week   ( )

5. How do you and your spouse feel about the frequency of your intercourse?

	Self	Spouse
a—Satisfied	( )	( )
b—Desire intercourse more frequently	( )	( )
c—Desire intercourse less frequently	( )	( )
d—Do not know	( )	( )

6–A. Are any of the following conditions affecting you and your spouse, so that you feel present sex activity is not representative? (Do not include aging or the passage of time.)

1—Pregnancy ( ) 7—Own or partner's health (mental or physical) ( )
2—Unusual job situation ( ) 8—Own or partner's interest in another person ( )
3—Separation (not due to marital friction) ( ) 9—Presence of children ( )
4—Separation (due to marital friction) ( ) 10—Personal or family crisis ( )
5—Marital friction ( ) 11—Other (specify) ( )
6—Housing ( ) 12—No (i.e., present sexual activity is representative ( )

6–B. If there are such conditions, how do you feel they affect your relationship?

1—For the better ( )
2—For the worse ( )
3—Neither better nor worse ( )

6–C. Approximately when did these conditions begin to affect your relationship?

1—Months ago ( )
2—Years ago ( )

6–D. Do you feel that there is a more typical frequency of intercourse than you reported in Question 4? If so, what is it?

1—No intercourse ( ) 6—3 times a week ( )
2—Less than once a month (specify) ( ) 7—4 times a week ( )
3—Once or twice a month ( ) 8—5 times a week ( )
4—Once a week ( ) 9—6 times a week ( )
5—Twice a week ( ) 10—7 times a week or more ( )
  11—If there is no frequency, check here ( )

7. What is the duration of sex play prior to penetration? (Be sure to answer, even if there is no penetration.)

Present		Past (if different)
( )	a—No sex play	( )
( )	b—Less than 10 minutes	( )
( )	c—10 min to less than 20 min	( )
( )	d—20 min to less than 30 min	( )
( )	e—30 min to less than 45 min	( )
( )	f—45 min to an hour	( )
( )	g—Over one hour	( )

8. How do you and your spouse feel about this duration of sex play?

Present			*Past (if different)*	
Self	*Spouse*		*Self*	*Spouse*
( )	( )	a—Satisfied	( )	( )
( )	( )	b—Desire longer sex play	( )	( )
( )	( )	c—Desire shorter sex play	( )	( )
( )	( )	d—Do not know	( )	( )

9. Average duration of penetration (include time before and after orgasm):

Present			*Past (if different)*	
Self	*Spouse*		*Self*	*Spouse*
( )	( )	a—No penetration	( )	( )
( )	( )	b—Less than 1 minute	( )	( )
( )	( )	c—1 to less than 5 min	( )	( )
( )	( )	d—5 to less than 10 min	( )	( )
( )	( )	e—10 to 20 min	( )	( )
( )	( )	f—Over 20 min (specify)	( )	( )

10. How do you and your spouse feel about this duration of penetration?

Present			*Past (if different)*	
Self	*Spouse*		*Self*	*Spouse*
( )	( )	a—Satisfied	( )	( )
( )	( )	b—Desire shorter time of penetration	( )	( )
( )	( )	c—Desire longer time of penetration	( )	( )
( )	( )	d—Do not know	( )	( )

11. Do you and your spouse have intercourse during menstrual period?

Present		*Past (if different)*
( )	a—Usually	( )
( )	b—Occasionally	( )
( )	c—Rarely	( )
( )	d—Never	( )
( )	e—No menstrual periods	( )

12. How do you each feel about intercourse during menstrual periods? (Give your feelings, whether you have intercourse at this time or not.)

Present		*Past (if different)*
( )	a—Feel the same as at other times	( )
( )	b—Dislike intercourse during menstruation	( )
( )	c—Prefer intercourse during menstruation	( )
( )	d—No objections, but believe it is harmful	( )
( )	e—Do not know	( )

13. During your sex activity together, does wife have orgasm?

Present		*Past (if different)*
( )	a—Always	( )
( )	b—Nearly always	( )
( )	c—About half the time	( )
( )	d—Seldom	( )
( )	e—Never	( )
( )	f—Do not know	( )

14. How do you and your spouse feel about frequency of wife's orgasm?

Present			*Past (if different)*	
Self	*Spouse*		*Self*	*Spouse*
( )	( )	a—Satisfied with frequency	( )	( )
( )	( )	b—Dissatisfied but not upset by it	( )	( )
( )	( )	c—Dissatisfied and upset by it	( )	( )
( )	( )	d—Do not know	( )	( )

15. Do you have more than one orgasm during a complete sex act (the period from start of arousal to end of activity connected with that arousal)? Does your spouse?

Present			*Past (if different)*	
Self	*Spouse*		*Self*	*Spouse*
( )	( )	a—No orgasm	( )	( )
( )	( )	b—Never more than 1 per act	( )	( )
( )	( )	c—Occasionally more than 1 per act	( )	( )
( )	( )	d—Frequently more than 1 per act	( )	( )
( )	( )	e—Do not know	( )	( )

16. When you or your spouse have orgasm during activity together, does it always occur by penetration?

Present			*Past (if different)*	
Self	*Spouse*		*Self*	*Spouse*
( )	( )	a—Always by penetration	( )	( )
( )	( )	b—Sometimes by penetration, sometimes by other means	( )	( )
( )	( )	c—Always by other means	( )	( )
( )	( )	d—No orgasm	( )	( )

17. If your own orgasm occurs by means other than penetration, how do you and your spouse each feel about this?

	Present			Past (if different)	
Self	*Spouse*			*Self*	*Spouse*
( )	( )	a—Not achieved by other means		( )	( )
( )	( )	b—Comfortable		( )	( )
( )	( )	c—Uncomfortable		( )	( )
( )	( )	d—Indifferent		( )	( )
( )	( )	e—Do not know		( )	( )

18. If your spouse's orgasm occurs by means other than penetration, how do you and your spouse each feel about this?

	Present			Past (if different)	
Self	*Spouse*			*Self*	*Spouse*
( )	( )	a—Not achieved by other means		( )	( )
( )	( )	b—Comfortable		( )	( )
( )	( )	c—Uncomfortable		( )	( )
( )	( )	d—Indifferent		( )	( )
( )	( )	e—Do not know		( )	( )

19. How frequently does it occur that your spouse desires intercourse and you do not?

Present		Past (if different)
( )	a—Frequently	( )
( )	b—Occasionally	( )
( )	c—Rarely	( )
( )	d—Never	( )
( )	e—Do not know when spouse desires intercourse	( )

20. How frequently does it occur that you desire intercourse and your spouse does not?

Present		Past (if different)
( )	a—Frequently	( )
( )	b—Occasionally	( )
( )	c—Rarely	( )
( )	d—Never	( )
( )	e—Do not know when spouse desires intercourse	( )

21. If you are not desirous, do you have intercourse to please your spouse?

Present		Past (if different)
( )	a—Frequently	( )
( )	b—Occasionally	( )
( )	c—Rarely	( )
( )	d—Never	( )
( )	e—Does not apply	( )

22. If your spouse is not desirous, does he/she have intercourse to please you?

Present		*Past (if different)*
( )	a—Frequently	( )
( )	b—Occasionally	( )
( )	c—Rarely	( )
( )	d—Never	( )
( )	e—Does not apply	( )
( )	f—Do not know	( )

23. In general, have you and your spouse been using any method of child spacing?

a—No Method	( )
b—Rhythm method ("safe period")	( )
c—Withdrawal	( )
d—Other methods	( )
e—Do not know	( )

24. Do you and your spouse feel secure about your method, or lack of method, of child spacing?

	Yourself	*Spouse*
a—Feel secure	( )	( )
b—Feel insecure	( )	( )
c—Do not know	( )	( )

25. Apart from security, how do you and your spouse feel about your method, or lack of method, of child spacing?

	Yourself	*Spouse*
a—Satisfied	( )	( )
b—Dissatisfied	( )	( )
c—Indifferent	( )	( )
d—Do not know	( )	( )

26. Can you and your spouse each discuss your feelings about sex freely with one another?

	Yourself	*Spouse*
a—Yes	( )	( )
b—No	( )	( )
c—About some things, not others	( )	( )
d—Do not know	( )	( )

Continued on following page:

27. Does your sex activity with your spouse include the following:

Frequency	Satisfaction with frequency	Feelings about this type of activity, whether or not you participate

A—GENERAL KISSING AND CARESSING

Present	Past		Self	Spouse		Self	Spouse
1—Always ( )	( )	1—Satisfied ( )	( )	1—Like ( )	( )
2—Usually ( )	( )	2—Dissatisfied ( )	( )	2—Dislike ( )	( )
3—Rarely ( )	( )	3—Indifferent ( )	( )	3—Mixed feelings ( )	( )
4—Never ( )	( )	4—Do not know ( )	( )	4—Indifferent ( )	( )
				5—Do not know ( )	( )

B—DEEP KISS

Present	Past		Self	Spouse		Self	Spouse
1—Always ( )	( )	1—Satisfied ( )	( )	1—Like ( )	( )
2—Usually ( )	( )	2—Dissatisfied ( )	( )	2—Dislike ( )	( )
3—Rarely ( )	( )	3—Indifferent ( )	( )	3—Mixed feelings ( )	( )
4—Never ( )	( )	4—Do not know ( )	( )	4—Indifferent ( )	( )
				5—Do not know ( )	( )

C—MANUAL MANIPULATION OF WIFE'S BREASTS

Present	Past		Self	Spouse		Self	Spouse
1—Always ( )	( )	1—Satisfied ( )	( )	1—Like ( )	( )
2—Usually ( )	( )	2—Dissatisfied ( )	( )	2—Dislike ( )	( )
3—Rarely ( )	( )	3—Indifferent ( )	( )	3—Mixed feelings ( )	( )
4—Never ( )	( )	4—Do not know ( )	( )	4—Indifferent ( )	( )
				5—Do not know ( )	( )

D—MOUTH MANIPULATION OF FEMALE GENITALIA

Present	Past		Self	Spouse		Self	Spouse
1—Always ( )	( )	1—Satisfied ( )	( )	1—Like ( )	( )
2—Usually ( )	( )	2—Dissatisfied ( )	( )	2—Dislike ( )	( )
3—Rarely ( )	( )	3—Indifferent ( )	( )	3—Mixed feelings ( )	( )
4—Never ( )	( )	4—Do not know ( )	( )	4—Indifferent ( )	( )
				5—Do not know ( )	( )

E—MOUTH MANIPULATION OF WIFE'S BREASTS

Present	Past		Self	Spouse		Self	Spouse
1—Always ( )	( )	1—Satisfied ( )	( )	1—Like ( )	( )
2—Usually ( )	( )	2—Dissatisfied ( )	( )	2—Dislike ( )	( )
3—Rarely ( )	( )	3—Indifferent ( )	( )	3—Mixed feelings ( )	( )
4—Never ( )	( )	4—Do not know ( )	( )	4—Indifferent ( )	( )
				5—Do not know ( )	( )

	Frequency	Satisfaction with frequency	Feelings about this type of activity, whether or not you participate

F—MANUAL MANIPULATION OF MALE GENITALIA

	Present	*Past*		*Self*	*Spouse*		*Self*	*Spouse*
1—Always	( )	( )	1—Satisfied	( )	( )	1—Like	( )	( )
2—Usually	( )	( )	2—Dissatisfied	( )	( )	2—Dislike	( )	( )
3—Rarely	( )	( )	3—Indifferent	( )	( )	3—Mixed feelings	( )	( )
4—Never	( )	( )	4—Do not know	( )	( )	4—Indifferent	( )	( )
						5—Do not know	( )	( )

G—ORAL CONTACT WITH FEMALE GENITALIA

	Present	*Past*		*Self*	*Spouse*		*Self*	*Spouse*
1—Always	( )	( )	1—Satisfied	( )	( )	1—Like	( )	( )
2—Usually	( )	( )	2—Dissatisfied	( )	( )	2—Dislike	( )	( )
3—Rarely	( )	( )	3—Indifferent	( )	( )	3—Mixed feelings	( )	( )
4—Never	( )	( )	4—Do not know	( )	( )	4—Indifferent	( )	( )
						5—Do not know	( )	( )

H—ORAL CONTACT WITH MALE GENITALIA

	Present	*Past*		*Self*	*Spouse*		*Self*	*Spouse*
1—Always	( )	( )	1—Satisfied	( )	( )	1—Like	( )	( )
2—Usually	( )	( )	2—Dissatisfied	( )	( )	2—Dislike	( )	( )
3—Rarely	( )	( )	3—Indifferent	( )	( )	3—Mixed feelings	( )	( )
4—Never	( )	( )	4—Do not know	( )	( )	4—Indifferent	( )	( )
						5—Do not know	( )	( )

J—ANAL PLAY

	Present	*Past*		*Self*	*Spouse*		*Self*	*Spouse*
1—Always	( )	( )	1—Satisfied	( )	( )	1—Like	( )	( )
2—Usually	( )	( )	2—Dissatisfied	( )	( )	2—Dislike	( )	( )
3—Rarely	( )	( )	3—Indifferent	( )	( )	3—Mixed feelings	( )	( )
4—Never	( )	( )	4—Do not know	( )	( )	4—Indifferent	( )	( )
						5—Do not know	( )	( )

K—OTHER SEXUAL ACTIVITY WITH SPOUSE

	Present	*Past*		*Self*	*Spouse*		*Self*	*Spouse*
1—Always	( )	( )	1—Satisfied	( )	( )	1—Like	( )	( )
2—Usually	( )	( )	2—Dissatisfied	( )	( )	2—Dislike	( )	( )
3—Rarely	( )	( )	3—Indifferent	( )	( )	3—Mixed feelings	( )	( )
4—Never	( )	( )	4—Do not know	( )	( )	4—Indifferent	( )	( )
						5—Do not know	( )	( )

28. What position(s) do you and your spouse use in intercourse?
    a—Male above, usually   ( )
    b—Female above, usually   ( )
    c—Male above and female above, equally   ( )
    d—Side by side   ( )
    e—Usually other positions   ( )

29. To what extent have you and your spouse experimented with positions?

    a—Never   ( )
    b—Occasionally   ( )
    c—Frequently   ( )

30. How do you and your spouse each feel about the position(s) you usually use?

	Yourself	Spouse
a—Satisfied	( )	( )
b—Dissatisfied	( )	( )
c—Indifferent	( )	( )
d—Do not know	( )	( )

31. Who usually takes the initiative in sex activity?
    a—Husband   ( )
    b—Wife   ( )
    c—Varies   ( )

32. Are there any questions pertaining to your sexual performance that you would like to discuss in person?
    a—Yes   ( )
    b—No   ( )

FOR FURTHER READING

1. American Medical Association. HUMAN SEXUALITY (Chicago, Ill.: AMA, 1972).
2. E. James Anthony. Communicating Therapeutically with Children, *Journal of the American Academy of Child Psychiatry* 3 (1964) 106-125.
3. D. W. Burnap. Sex Education in the Physician's Office, *Pediatric Clinics of North America* 16, 2 (1969) 497-503.
4. D. W. Burnap & J. S. Golden. Sexual Problems in Medical Practice, *Journal of Medical Education* 42 (1967) 673-680.
5. Mary Calderone, Ed. MANUAL OF FAMILY PLANNING AND CONTRACEPTIVE PRACTICE, 2nd ed (Baltimore, Md.: Williams & Wilkins, 1970).
*6. Allen J. Enelow & Murray Wexler. PSYCHIATRY IN THE PRACTICE OF MEDICINE (New York: Oxford Univ. Press, 1966).
7. Group for the Advancement of Psychiatry. THE DIAGNOSTIC PROCESS IN CHILD PSYCHIATRY, GAP Report No. 38 (New York: GAP, 1957).
8. ———. SEX AND THE COLLEGE STUDENT, GAP Report No. 60 (New York: GAP, 1965).
9. ———. NORMAL ADOLESCENCE, GAP Report No. 68 (New York: GAP, 1968).
10. Saul I. Harrison. "Communicating with Children in Psychotherapy," in COMMUNICATION IN CLINICAL PRACTICE, R. W. Waggoner & D. J. Carek, eds (International Psychiatry Clinics) (Boston, Mass.: Little, Brown & Co., 1964) pp 39-51.
11. H. A. Katchadourian & D. T. Lunde. FUNDAMENTALS OF HUMAN SEXUALITY (New York: Holt, Rinehart & Winston, 1972).
12. A. C. Kinsey, W. B. Pomeroy & C. S. Martin. SEXUAL BEHAVIOR IN THE HUMAN MALE (Philadelphia, Pa.: W. B. Saunders, 1948).
13. ———. SEXUAL BEHAVIOR IN THE HUMAN FEMALE (Philadelphia, Pa.: W. B. Saunders, 1953).
14. R. H. Klemer. COUNSELING IN MARITAL AND SEXUAL PROBLEMS (Baltimore, Md.: Williams & Wilkins, 1965).
15. Harold I. Lief. Sex Education of Medical Students and Doctors, *Pacific Medicine & Surgery* 73 (1965) 52-58.
16. ———. The Physician and Family Planning, *Journal of the American Medical Association* 197, 8 (1966) 646-650.
17. ———. New Developments in the Sex Education of the Physician, *Journal of the American Medical Association* 212 (1970) 1864-1867.
18. ———. "Medical Aspects of Sexuality," in CECIL-LOEB TEXTBOOK OF MEDICINE, T. B. Beeson & W. McDermott eds (Philadelphia, Pa.: W. B. Saunders, 1971).

* Asterisked entries furnish the reader additional discussion about interviewing and interviewing technique.

19. Harold I. Lief & R. C. Fox. "Training for 'Detached Concern' in Medical Students," in THE PSYCHOLOGICAL BASIS OF MEDICAL PRACTICE (New York: Hoeber Medical Division, Harper & Row, 1963) pp 12-35.

20. F. J. Margolis. Preparing Parents and the Community, *Pediatric Clinics of North America* 16, 2 (1969) 471-485.

21. W. H. Masters & V. E. Johnson. HUMAN SEXUAL RESPONSE (Boston, Mass.: Little, Brown & Co., 1966).

22. ———. HUMAN SEXUAL INADEQUACY (Boston, Mass.: Little, Brown & Co., 1970).

23. J. L. McCary. HUMAN SEXUALITY (Princeton, N. J.: D. Van Nostrand, 1967).

*24. W. L. Morgan, Jr. & G. L. Engel. THE CLINICAL APPROACH TO THE PATIENT (Philadelphia, Pa.: W. B. Saunders, 1969).

25. E. M. Nash, L. N. Jessner & D. W. Abse, Eds. MARRIAGE COUNSELING IN MEDICAL PRACTICE (Chapel Hill, N. C.: Univ. of North Carolina Press, 1964) .

26. H. A. Otto. "Premarital Counseling," in COUNSELING IN MARITAL AND SEXUAL PROBLEMS, R. H. Klemer, ed (Baltimore, Md.: Williams & Wilkins, 1965) 258-268.

27. I. B. Pauly. Human Sexuality in Medical Education and Practice, *Australian & New Zealand Journal of Psychiatry* 5, 3 (1971).

28. E. Pfeiffer, A. Verwoerdt & G. C. Davis. Sexual Behavior in Middle Life, *American Journal of Psychiatry* 128 (1972) 82-87.

29. I. L. Reiss. THE SOCIAL CONTEXT OF PREMARITAL SEXUAL PERMISSIVENESS (New York: Holt, Rinehart & Winston, 1967) .

30. A. L. Rutledge. PREMARITAL COUNSELING (Cambridge, Mass.: Schenkman Publishing, 1966).

*31. Ian Stevenson. THE DIAGNOSTIC INTERVIEW, 2nd ed (New York: Harper & Row, 1971).

32. University of Minnesota. PROGRAM IN HUMAN SEXUALITY (Chicago, Ill.: Playboy Press, 1972).

*33. Kerr L. White et al. MANUAL FOR THE EXAMINATION OF PATIENTS (Chicago, Ill.: Year Book Medical Publishers, 1960) .

ACKNOWLEDGMENTS TO CONTRIBUTORS

The program of the Group for the Advancement of Psychiatry, a nonprofit, tax-exempt organization, is made possible largely through the voluntary contributions and efforts of its members. For their financial assistance during the past fiscal year, in helping it to fulfill its aims, GAP is grateful to the following:

Sponsors
CIBA–GEIGY Corporation, Pharmaceuticals Division
The Commonwealth Fund
The Division Fund
Maurice Falk Medical Fund
The Finkelstein Foundation
The Grant Foundation
The Grove Foundation
The Holzheimer Fund
Ittleson Family Foundation
The Olin Foundation
Reader's Digest Foundation
A. H. Robins Company
Roche Laboratories
Sandoz Pharmaceuticals
Schering Corporation
Mrs. Sylvia Schwartz
The Murray L. Silberstein Fund
The Lucille Ellis Simon Foundation
The Norton Simon Foundation
The Smart Family Foundation
Smith Kline & French Laboratories
van Ameringen Foundation, Inc.
Lawrence Weinberg
Wyeth Laboratories

Donors
Virginia & Nathan Bederman Foundation
Harper & Row, Publishers
Orrin Stine
The Stone Foundation, Inc.